Life Is a Joke

ROSEMARY FRIEDMAN was educated at Queen's College, Harley Street, and University College, London. She has published twenty-four titles and many of her twenty novels have been widely translated and serialised by the BBC. Her short stories have been syndicated worldwide. She has written commissioned screenplays (UK and US) and television scripts, and has judged a number of literary prizes. Her three stage plays all had successful runs. She is married to psychiatrist Dennis Friedman (*An Unsolicited Gift*, Arcadia 2010) and lives in London. She is a Fellow of PEN (Executive Committee 1993–1998); member of Bafta; member of the Writers' Guild; member of the Royal Society of Literature and member of the Society of Authors (Executive Committee 1989–1992). www.rosemaryfriedman.co.uk

OTHER TITLES BY ROSEMARY FRIEDMAN

FICTION

No White Coat	*Love On My List*
We All Fall Down	*Patients of a Saint*
The Fraternity	*The Commonplace Day*
The General Practice	*Practice Makes Perfect*
The Life Situation	*The Long Hot Summer*
Proofs of Affection	*A Loving Mistress*
Rose of Jericho	*A Second Wife*
To Live in Peace	*An Eligible Man*
Golden Boy	*Vintage*
Intensive Care	*Paris Summer*

NON-FICTION
The Writing Game
A Writer's Commonplace Book

JUVENILE
Aristide
Aristide in Paris

ROSEMARY FRIEDMAN

Life Is a Joke

A WRITER'S MEMOIR

ARCADIA BOOKS

Arcadia Books Ltd
15–16 Nassau Street
London W1W 7AB

www.arcadiabooks.co.uk

First published by Arcadia Books 2010

A catalogue record for this book is available from the British Library.

ISBN 978-1-906413-81-1

Typeset in Minion by MacGuru Ltd
Printed and bound in the UK by CPI Mackays, Chatham ME5 8TD

Arcadia Books gratefully acknowledges the financial support of Arts Council England.

Arcadia Books supports English PEN, the fellowship of writers who work together to promote literature and its understanding. English PEN upholds writers' freedoms in Britain and around the world, challenging political and cultural limits on free expression. To find out more, visit www.englishpen.org or contact English PEN, 6–8 Amwell Street, London EC1R 1UQ

Arcadia Books distributors are as follows:

in the UK and elsewhere in Europe:
Turnaround Publishers Services
Unit 3, Olympia Trading Estate
Coburg Road
London N22 6TZ

in the US and Canada:
Dufour Editions
PO Box 7
Chester Springs
PA, 19425

in Australia:
The Scribo Group Pty Ltd
18 Rodborough Road
Frenchs Forest 2086

in New Zealand:
Addenda
PO Box 78224
Grey Lynn
Auckland

in South Africa:
Jacana Media (Pty) Ltd
PO Box 291784,
Melville 2109
Johannesburg

Arcadia Books is the *Sunday Times* Small Publisher of the Year

Life is a joke that's just begun!

W. S. Gilbert

Finding myself quite empty, with nothing to write about, I offered myself to myself as theme and subject matter.

Michel de Montaigne

A man who gives a good account of himself is probably lying, since any life when viewed from the inside is simply a series of defeats.

George Orwell

For

Emily
Henry
Jack
George
Barnaby
Miranda
Savanna
Isabelle
Mia
Joel

Contents

1. Are You Still Writing? 1
2. The Writing on the Wall 12
3. Cancer Ward 21
4. Dead Letter Perfect 33
5. The Casting Couch 43
6. Déjà Vu 55
7. Old Geysers 66
8. Things 78
9. The Bottom Line 87
10. Idiot Box 97
11. Change of Heart 109
12. Deep in the Heart of Texas 119
13. My Grandmother's Chicken Soup 129
14. The Dinner Party Book 139
15. Paris Summer 149
16. The Human Condition 158
17. All Mod. Con. 168
18. Start Right 178
19. Character Arc 188
20. Family Reunion 197
21. The Golden Mask 207
22. Feeling and Thinking 218

Acknowledgements 228

Are You Still Writing?

Golden lads and girls all must
As chimney sweepers come to dust.

WILLIAM SHAKESPEARE

One of the creepiest stories in Greek myth is that of Tithonus, an ordinary man, who caught the eye of the goddess Eos. She begged the gods to grant him immortality so that she could be with him for ever. Unfortunately she forgot to ask for eternal youth and the gods did not offer it, so Tithonus grew older and older until eventually he was so wrinkled and shrunken that he turned into a cicada, which presumably lived for ever.

Being asked the question 'Are you still writing?' reminds one that in the mind of the questioner, at least, the writing is on the wall. 'Would that God the gift had gi' us to see ourselves as others see us'. But he/she hasn't. The psyche does not age. Inside we feel no different from how we felt at five, at fifteen, at twenty-five and so on down the decades and although we may scarcely recognise the image of ourselves reflected in the mirror, we regard with some surprise the fact that the questioner has had the temerity to ask at all. We live longer. While some inhabitants of the high mountain valley of Vilcabamba in South America, the Okinawans, and the Hunza from the mountains of Pakistan (what is it with mountains?) have a reputation for achieving longevity, many cultures – such as the Sumerians and the Indus Valley – document groups of people who have lived for hundreds of years. Methuselah, according to the book of Genesis, made it to 969. Official life expectancy in the UK is currently 78.4 years for a woman and seventy-six years for a man (forty per cent less had we been born in Swaziland) and the Census Bureau has predicted that in the year 2100 the United States will have 5.3 million people over the age of a hundred. In the UK, too, the future looks 'grey'. For the first time the number of pensioners, one in five of the total population, exceeds the number of children, and practical measures are called for, such as designing houses with fewer steps, doors wide enough to take wheelchairs and electricity sockets installed at waist level. Even as we speak, Britain faces a time bomb of age-related dementia (700,000 in the UK alone) although according to a caustic Doris Lessing 'people decide to be old'.

Yes, I am 'still' writing. Even if we accept that our bodies can't last for ever, nobody wants to spend his/her latter years as a shrunken grasshopper. We seriously want to keep our minds intact. The question, however, with its element of surprise at confronting the lines on your face and your silver hair, contains within it the thinly disguised amazement at the fact that not only are you 'still' writing but that you are 'still' alive. It is no consolation to know that the death rate for the human race is never less than one hundred per cent.

The skeletons of 17,000 previous inhabitants of London, which were uncovered by workmen's spades or mechanical diggers from cemeteries and burial pits (for the unfortunate victims of the plague), are held in the collections of the

Museum of London. The most interesting of these remains were carefully curated and displayed in an exhibition at the Wellcome Collection, which enabled visitors to build up a clear picture of each individual's age and sex, an idea of the work he did and the food he ate, the deprivations he experienced, and the diseases from which he suffered, many of which were finally eradicated with the advent of vaccination. Examination of the bones, by skilled osteologists brought each individual's story of syphilis, rickets or multiple myeloma to life. As we drift, in the half-light, through the reassembled bodies in their glass sarcophagi, we see the horrendous results of untreated dental decay and picture the devastating effects of smallpox, described by Samuel Pepys as being 'as common as swearing or eating' and a hazard for everyone regardless of class or income. Gazing upon the unequivocal evidence of the Bubonic Plague, we shudder to think that millions of erstwhile city dwellers lie immolated beneath what are today Pizza Huts, car parks and shopping centres, and that what were once their resting places have long been incorporated into the fabric of London, turned into streets or railways or planted with trees and flowers to provide parks and playgrounds. In the face of this uncompromising foretaste of the future, this ghoulish confirmation of the fact that life is a terminal disease, I am reminded that like Montaigne – who prayed that Death would find him 'planting his cabbages' – I have never written a book or play without thinking that I might die before the work was completed. As far as the small print is concerned, however, I should prefer my life to be snuffed out 'under general anaesthetic as if it were a diseased appendix'.*

I have always been fascinated by the thousand-year-old

---

* Richard Dawkins, *The God Delusion*, 2006

story of the Baghdad merchant who sent his servant out to buy provisions. In the market the servant bumps into a woman whom he recognises as Death. Terrified, he rushes home and pleads for the loan of his master's horse in order to flee to Samarra where Death will never find him. The master agrees and the servant takes himself off. The master himself then goes down to the market where he bumps into Death and chastises her for frightening his servant. 'Oh,' says Death, 'I didn't mean to frighten him, I was just surprised to find him in Baghdad this morning when I have an appointment with him tonight in Samarra.'

It is a spooky story, which mimics our own efforts, in particular as our lives draw to an inevitable close, to defeat death and regard with some degree of *Schadenfreude* the demise of those taken in comparative youth, of contemporaries whether known or not known: 'Light aircraft crashes, killing five'; 'Stabbing attack leaves teenager dead'.

'Any man's death diminishes me.' A friend is dying. He knows but does not want to know. He eats nothing. Keeps nothing down. Is getting progressively thin, progressively weak. In a fortnight he will go fishing. Or so he says. His powers are waning. We know that he will not have the strength to cast the bait, to hold the rod, to make the journey. He prepares his flies in their rusty tin. We go along with the charade. Talk of other things. It is the way he wants it. Who is to say otherwise?

Who is to challenge the obituaries with their mendacious photographs, taken in the flower of their youth, of eighty- or ninety-year-olds who have keeled over without preamble or succumbed to long illnesses 'bravely born' or 'battled with' – as if cancer came at you fully armed and you had any choice in the matter.

We turn guiltily to the relevant pages, appropriately situated near the end of the newspaper (to remark the lifespans, to reassure ourselves that it is not yet our turn, that we have, for today at least, been let off the hook), become past masters at decoding the subtext: 'He never married' (gay); 'Did not suffer fools gladly' (arrogant); 'Could be bearish and candid' (disagreeable). Ashes to ashes and dust to dust: a lifetime of schools attended and degrees received, of vocations and hobbies, of military service and memberships, of accomplishments and passions and glittering prizes culminating suddenly or lingeringly in, at best, half a page of newsprint and a memorial fund, or, at worst, a glass vase (choice of six colours), necklace or paperweight fashioned in Billericay from your cremated remains.

Yes, I am still writing. Despite the fact that there were more than half a million books on offer at this year's London Book Fair, vending machines are churning out novels, e-books are the new paperbacks and traditional bookshops are closing; notwithstanding the fact that a price war is raging between a powerful online bookseller (which accounts for sixteen per cent of all book sales in Britain and which already buys its books at half the cover price) and a leading publisher; regardless of evidence that authors are caught in the crossfire and are losing vital royalties from supermarkets where popular titles vie (pricewise) with tins of baked beans and washing-up liquid, where Harry Potter sells for £1, and where browsers in those independent bookshops that remain sneak out to buy their books cheaper online. High fees demanded by the powerful chain booksellers – £45,000 to puff certain titles at Christmas, £25,000 to display a 'gift book' at the till, and £17,000 for 'offer of the week' – do little to promote a wider range of quality books, especially if you consider that a war of attrition is in progress and that if a publisher refuses to play ball with these outrageous demands his orders go down not from 1,000 to 500 copies of a title but to a paltry twenty!

The new contender, from technology, in the shape of a reading device that could engender a publishing revolution as far reaching as William Caxton's with his printing press, is yet another indication that the book industry is looking for new ways to distribute and sell books. The electronic book, roughly the size of an average paperback, with its 200 megabytes of memory, is capable of storing 160 books of average length. Readers of books, however, *like* books and by no means solely for their capacity to 'furnish a room'. I am no exception and my shelves, jealously guarded – for a bibliophile losing a book is more traumatic than losing a friend and I *never* lend them – are lined with books I have hankered after, bought, read and annotated for future reference. The attachment to the traditional volume grows with time as the book begins to bear the traces of the owner's personality, of the hands that touched it. Will the neat package, the size of a wallet, now on offer have the same emotional value? Apparently 'oldie-friendly', the digital reader will be a boon to people who find a small typeface anathema and because of its reduced publishing costs it will benefit authors by enabling them to see their work published even if they are catering for a minority audience. Publishers are promising to make thousands of titles available and estimate that digital books will account for one per cent of sales by the end of the decade. Whether the new e-books, which I have a sneaking feeling will appeal to gadget lovers rather than book lovers, will ever be downloaded in sufficient numbers (notwithstanding the fact that theoretically you could take six heavy tomes away in your holiday suitcase) to kill off the book as we know it, with its comforting spine and cover, and its visceral appeal, has yet to be decided. The jury is out. To the writer this technological advance would seem to make little difference. Our task is to write and the way in which our words are ultimately dished up and consumed is of secondary importance.

We do not write because we want to, we write because we must. As Francis Bacon commented: 'We are born and we die, but in between we give this purposeless existence a meaning by our drives.' Writing, like falling in love, is a pathological state. There is no option. It is what we do and what we are. For the writer there is no question of a second career, flower arranging, or joining a choir and singing madrigals. Given a modicum of health, the twilight years could turn out to be every bit as important in defining our lives, in perfecting our work, putting the official stamp on it, as youth and middle age.

'Are you still writing?' is usually followed by 'Are you still living at …?' with its sinister implication of retirement home or sheltered housing. It was a neighbour who persuaded us, long before we needed it, that we would not always be able to cope with the physical demands of a house on five floors. Ten years ago, and in what we mistakenly thought was still our prime, we laughed him out of court. Not long afterwards, in response to estate agents' particulars that mysteriously began to come through the door, we began to look at flats. Not seriously, mind: after a series of family houses with gardens, who could contemplate living on one comparatively minuscule and boring level with no outside space? Other people's homes, like other people's lives, reflected their lifestyles and had no bearing on our own. Paying lip service to their box-like rooms and their alien *modi vivendi* – we were not flat dwellers after all – we wondered where we would stash our boxes of papers, our thousands of books, our computers and printers in what passed for living space but was not how we lived. There is more than one death: one's childhood, one's youth, one's middle, and often most productive, years.

We sold the house with its lares and penates and its happy memories, and mourned the passing of our 'young old age' in an apartment we stumbled upon, which was blessed not only with 'outside space' but with room, beneath the eaves, to store the piles of manuscripts (umpteen drafts) and old lever-arch files and receipts and playbills and unsold copies of novels unwisely purchased from the publishers and desiccated cans of paint (in case any touching up was needed) and inextricably tangled spare leads for technical equipment long extinct, and dusty hampers of family photographs and slides, which had accumulated over the years. The move, traumatic as it seemed at the time, has not proved bad and the well-meaning neighbour has been proved right. We could not have managed the five floors for very much longer.

Although today no one in his/her right mind thinks that life is over just because one is eighty, there is no escaping the gradual but inevitable loss of strength and independence that accompany the ageing process. No one tells you, when you are young – why should they rain on your parade? – just how painful old age can be: the aching morning body, the difficulties of getting up from low chairs, the inability to hold fast to minuscule items. Physical infirmity creeps up, advances so slowly that you hardly notice it. Stairs that were once taken two at a time, with no help from a supporting banister, become obstacles to be surmounted with as much fortitude as a cliff face and with similar strain upon capricious knees. There are stairs in our apartment (a 'duplex' in estate agent speak) and few though they may be they are no laughing matter. Recently, although hard to say when, unmentionable words such as 'stairlift' and 'grab handles' have begun to be heard. They will spoil the decor; put the stamp of reality on lives that, astonishingly to those in possession of them, have hardly begun. For that's what it seems like.

When did you lose the zip and the energy, the ability to move like a panther and run like the hind? Even if you have had the good luck not to be afflicted with macular degeneration or heart disease, when did a common or garden step become an obstacle, low-pitched sounds recede into inaudibility and the glare of the lights from oncoming traffic, in which we are still lucky enough to be driving (according to Age Concern 'older drivers are some of the safest on the road') dazzle and blind? No matter how assiduous our vigil, we cannot pinpoint the moment when a daffodil opens, watch the golden trumpet unfurl from tight green bud; we cannot capture the passing of time, quantify the inexorable metamorphosis into dotage. That's all right. In our increasingly frequent 'senior moments' we might be unable to remember where all the days have gone but at least we know that we have seized them.

Hard on the heels of 'Are you still writing?' and 'Are you still in the same house?' comes a further enquiry containing the pregnant 'still'. 'Is your husband still …?' What the questioner is trying to establish is whether you are still part of a couple or are a widow discreetly 'looking for friendship, companionship, or even love …' from a 'delightful, well-matured man', 'a friendly quiet widower planning a move to France', or a 'personable, tall gentleman', plucked from the Getting Together columns of *The Oldie*. My husband and I are extremely lucky. The long-service medals, Ruby, Golden, Diamond, superseding the platinum of the wedding band, have been duly presented on the appropriate anniversaries and, in the shape of rings, adorn my fingers on high days and holidays. Where is the defeat here? If we are honest with ourselves we know that, like the perfect car and the perfect holiday, there is no such thing as a 'perfect' marriage. How utterly boring that would be. There have been times when we have toyed with the idea of divorce (or murder), times when the wheels of cohabitation have squeaked for want of oil. When the chips were down, however, as they sometimes are in every partnership, 'we loved and laughed and cried, and did it our way'. The storms have subsided. We have entered waters so calm, so pacific, we wish them to go on for ever. Yes, my husband is 'still ...' As I look at the daily increasing number of widows around me and think there but for the grace of a God, in whom I no longer believe, go I and hope that my number is called before his and that after so many years of the kind of happiness to which many aspire and few are granted, I will not be required to go it alone.

'Make room for others as others have made room for you.'* As far as dying is concerned no one, even in the condemned cell, even hearing the sound of his friends and comrades being shot, ever really believes in his own death nor can he imagine it. If we try to do so we realise that we are still present as spectators.

As far as 'facing it' is concerned, it is a daily exercise

---

* Montaigne

particularly when it comes to wondering how long we will be around to see the launch, and success or failure, of our current projects, the trajectories of grandchildren at their various and exciting stages on the ladder. We know that life has been good to us. We are greedy. We want it to go on, at least until we are incapable of converting life into fiction through novels, plays and short stories, of filling up the bin bags of our writers' minds from the smouldering rubbish heaps of experience, from everything we think and see and feel and notice around us, and trying to make coherent and significant arrangements of them. Time, the great scavenger, is no longer the ally but an enemy; not a benefactor but a creditor, systematically destroying first this faculty then that, liquidating the wisdom, destroying the images, the unique private collection – the friends and acquaintances, the triumphs and the failures, the homes and the holidays, the cafés and the concerts, the memories and the music, the bridges and the beaches, the laughter and the learning, the pomp and the circumstance – that is the human personality. Often I catch myself wondering what I am going to do 'when I grow up'. I am not alone. With very few exceptions life ceases for us just when we are getting ready for it. A few years ago mine took a nasty and unexpected jolt when I had my brush with Death but, unlike in the fable, the messenger did not, on that occasion, follow me to Samarra.

2

The Writing on the Wall

Even though I walk through the valley of the shadow ...
PSALM 23

There is a ring binder in my study that I never open in case, like Lot's wife, I am turned into the proverbial pillar of salt. I open it now. Reluctantly. It has a profoundly depressing effect on me, even after five years. The label on the spine of the file gives the date of my *annus horribilis* together with the word 'Lungs'. They are only part of the story.

My second play, *Change of Heart*, was based on the tragic shortage of donor organs for those whose hearts and lungs are failing, and in particular on the bizarre circumstances of Professor (now Dame) Julia Polak who was found to be suffering from the very disease she was researching. The play was produced in the winter of 2004 at the New End Theatre, Hampstead, where it had a successful six-week run. As the run drew to a close I began to feel more and more ill, and had increasing difficulty in dragging myself up the steep Hampstead hill towards the theatre. As the applause reverberated and the cast (which included Julie-Kate Olivier, daughter of Sir Laurence) took their final bow, I found myself faint, dripping with perspiration and almost too weak to stand. I put it down to the heat of the theatre, which by the laws of thermodynamics rose to where I always had my seat in the back row. With the passing of the days, and the heady excitement of seeing one's characters come to life on the stage fading, my health began to deteriorate and the daily round became more onerous. After an episode of severe mid-back pain, which came on suddenly one Saturday, I was taken to the local A&E where I queued up to see a nervous and delightful, newly qualified houseman who dismissed the pain as muscular, prescribed four-hourly analgesics and reassured me that it would be better by Monday.

It was not. After a weekend of high temperatures and rigors, I was sent by my GP to a chest physician, who for obvious reasons will remain nameless. I was diagnosed with 'right upper-lobe pneumonia', which did not need hospitalisation but was treated with the appropriate drugs. When the symptoms subsided, I made another appointment, as requested, with the chest physician and this time was accompanied by my youngest daughter, a consultant radiologist. When the X-rays of my chest were shown to her on the light box her expression changed. Pointing to a section of the film, she indicated that although the 'pneumonia' had resolved, all was far from well. From that moment on I was on a macabre roller-coaster I could well have done without and from which it was going to take me a long and arduous time to alight.

Chest X-rays at the Royal London Hospital, where my daughter worked, revealed a 'mass arising from the right hilum suggestive of a primary lung neoplasm ...' Although I was not, and had never been, a smoker, lung cancer was confirmed by a PET scan performed at the specialist London Imaging Centre. PET stands for Positron Emission

Tomography, which is an imaging technique that, together with X-rays, uses small quantities of a radiation tracer to produce pictures showing the density of different organs in the body. Combining these two techniques in one scanner provides important information that will affect future treatment.

After fasting for six hours, except for drinking copious amounts of water, which helps to flush the tracer through the body, a vein is injected with radioactive sugar and, once this has been absorbed, you are slid into the scanner from which, after sixty surreal minutes, the requisite images will have been collected.

The findings of the PET scan were '... strongly support-ive of a primary lung malignancy' although, fortunately, this information was left to the chest physician to impart to me and, in accordance with protocol, was not given to me at the time.

Lung cancer, poetically described as 'a disease of the soul', is one of the most difficult cancers to treat and has one of the lowest survival outcomes of any type of cancer. Only about twenty people out of a hundred will live for one year after diagnosis, six out of a hundred for at least five years, and a paltry five out of a hundred for ten years. For those who have surgery to remove their cancer only twenty patients out of a hundred are alive five years later, a complication being where the tumour has spread to the lymph nodes.

Happily, I was unaware of these statistics when, together with my husband and radiologist daughter, I went back to the chest physician to be told the results of the PET scan and the recent lung-function test (spirometry).

Spirometry, meaning the measuring of breath, is the most common of the Pulmonary Function Tests (PFTs). It measures specifically the amount (volume) and/or speed (flow) of air that can be inhaled and exhaled. The patient, with clips on her nostrils to prevent air escaping through the nose, is asked to take the deepest possible breath and then exhale into the sensor (a wide plastic tube inserted into the mouth) as hard as possible. Since the result of the test was highly dependent upon the co-operation of the patient, I inhaled and exhaled as hard as possible, almost busting a gut in the process, as if it were some examination in which I was aiming for distinction. Needless to say the results were not divulged to me at the end of the manoeuvre and despite my Herculean efforts I did not know whether I had passed the test and had no idea of my marks.

We had to wait. In the chest physician's gloomy waiting room. Until my name was called. A black posse of Middle-Eastern ladies, accompanied by an interpreter and with only their eyes visible through the slits of their enveloping burkhas, was ushered into the sanctum sanctorum first. The wait was intolerable. We did not speak. We flicked blindly through time-expired copies of *Country Life* and did not meet each other's eyes. When the Middle-Eastern delegation had filed out, the physician himself came out of his room to summon us. It was a bad sign. Longing, yet not longing, to cut to the chase, we exchanged pleasantries. No, it was no longer raining. Yes, the winter had been cold and there were few signs of spring. He put the latest X-ray films up on the light box, fidgeted with his lapels, rearranged the papers on his desk, which already looked pretty tidy. 'Yes,' he said finally, 'there was some malignancy in the right lung.' He pointed out the tumour to my daughter whose eyes had not left the light box and who had already summed up the situation for herself.

The consultant said he was sorry. For keeping us waiting? For messing up the diagnosis in the first place? For the fact that outside the confines of his consulting room with its purring air-conditioning unit, there were few signs of spring? The bad news having been imparted, he was back on track. The diagnosis, following the PET scan and more chest X-rays than I have had hot dinners, was a primary lung malignancy. Surgery was a 'possibility' if the lymph nodes in the lung were not affected, in which case a Mr Goldstraw at the Royal Brompton Hospital was my man.

I don't remember how we got home, only that it was in silence as we digested the news that I had lung cancer with all its dire implications. My irrational fears suddenly appeared to have become reality as I guessed that I would not live to publish my current book. In the flat (the duplex), we went our separate ways. Our daughter, hardened medic as she was, into the sitting room to shed a quiet tear, and I, shedding my own noisy ones at the thought that my life was to be so soon curtailed, into my husband's comforting arms.

Psychological theories of illness are a powerful means of placing the blame on the ill. It was not the naming of the disease that was demoralising but the common perception that 'cancer' – always an emotive word – was an invincible predator. The disease is sometimes regarded as a form of demonic possession, which is not helped by the fact that tumours are categorised as 'malignant' or 'benign', leading many people to put their trust in faith healers whose optimistic and misguided aim is to 'correct the imbalance' in the body.

I felt like Solzhenitsyn's Pavel Nikolayevich who wondered why '… unforeseen and unprepared for, the disease had come upon him, a happy man with few cares, like a gale in the space of two weeks'. What was I to do? I pinned my hopes on the quaintly named Mr Goldstraw, who surely would be able to 'make it better', to cut the tumour out.

The waiting room at the Royal Brompton Hospital was filled with families who had accompanied their loved ones to their oncology appointments. Stick-thin men and anxious women read tattered magazines or sat in agonised silence as unhealthy-looking children played with crayons and boxes of tired plastic toys.

The charming Mr Goldstraw had my X-rays on his desk. Yes, I had a primary lung malignancy. Nothing new here. A lot of silence was broken by my optimistic query as to how soon he could excise it. He looked shifty. Muttered something I could not quite catch but knew that it had something to do with lymph nodes and infiltration across something-or-other and into something-or-other, which might make the surgical procedure difficult if not impossible. The bottom line was that there were to be more X-rays (an excess of these alone could give you cancer) and more investigations before he could make up his mind about the possibility of surgery.

The 'investigations', about the precise nature of which I had no idea at the time, turned out to mean entering a Hieronymus Bosch world of living hell upon which my team of husband and four daughters, unfailing in their support, could only look with thinly disguised anguish.

It is not always possible to tell conclusively from imaging tests, such as the ones I had already undergone, the exact nature of a lesion nor even, conclusively, whether it is benign or cancerous. A bronchoscopy, followed by a non-surgical biopsy, which involved removing some cells from any suspicious area within the body and examining them under a microscope to make a final diagnosis, so that treatment planning could begin, were prescribed.

A bronchoscopy consists of a bronchoscope or fibre-optic telescope, as thick as a pencil, being passed through the nose, down the back of the throat, into the windpipe and down into the bronchi. It allows light to shine round bends so that the inside of the airways can be seen clearly. It is used to diagnose cancer of the bronchus (lung cancer). I was glad to hear that only in one of a hundred bronchoscopies did serious complications occur. Apart from a miserable soreness of the throat, a painful cough and a high temperature for a day or two, I quickly recovered and pressed the 'delete' key on the whole unpleasant experience the result of which was 'no result', a full biopsy apparently having been precluded by the bleeding lateral segment of the right mid-lobe.

A 'needle biopsy' followed. They do not tell you that the needle used to reach the suspected lesion is not, as one might imagine, a fine-gauge one such as is used to draw blood, but is several inches long with a barrel about as wide as a large paper clip. This 'needle', which is hollow, is connected to a trough, or shallow receptacle, covered by a sheath and is attached to a spring-loaded mechanism. With the patient wide awake and lying on her back, a small nick is made in the skin at the site where the core needle is to be inserted and, using imaging guidance, the physician (a specially trained interventional radiologist) inserts the needle through the skin, advances it to the site of the nodule and, in theory at least, removes samples of tissue.

Although the pain of piercing the chest wall and searching for the obstruction was intense, the instruction, which one was scared to disobey, was to lie still and not to cough during the procedure. Terrified to move, and ordered to hold my breath when requested to do so, I had no idea, after the first foray through the chest wall and into the lung, that several attempts would be made nor that more than one specimen would be needed for complete analysis. The radiologist, not the most chatty of operators, had his back to me after the needle was withdrawn and pressure was applied by a nurse to stop the bleeding. I had the impression, as he fiddled with his syringes and glass bottles on a side table, that something was amiss. It was a painful and traumatic experience and as I was wheeled up to the ward where I was to be monitored for possible complications, I was glad that the investigation was over and that I would not have to undergo such a miserable procedure again. How wrong I was. The radiologist had *missed* the target and no sooner was I was home again and recovering in my own bed than I was telephoned by the hospital to say that not only had the procedure to be repeated but that it was to be carried out the next day. I don't know whether or not it was because of my now weakened state, but I said that I was not going to go, and burst into tears.

Of course I went. By way of a change, I lay on my front and the radiologist, to do him justice, full of apologies, inserted the needle from the back. This time the procedure not only did not produce the required amount of tissue from the right place but provoked an unpleasant and copious haemoptysis (coughing up of blood) the trajectory of which he managed to dodge (leaving mopping-up operations to the nurses) but a painful and collapsed mid-lobe of the lung (more X-rays and a tube inserted into the chest) which to this day has not recovered. Yet again, the required amount of cells had not been aspirated. Weak from the haemoptysis, I could not believe my ears. I was sent home to recover before the next bout, which was to be handed over to a more senior and dextrous physician. Third time lucky, although with no less discomfort during which I was several times reassured that it was 'nearly over' when it was not. The 'eureka' moment was followed by a long hiatus during which the rogue cells were sent away to a histopathology laboratory for examination and report. During this time the plot, which was to become more and more complicated, thickened. The histology findings were passed from one expert in the field to another and from supplementary report to supplementary report. Did I, or did I not, have lung cancer? Should I be putting my affairs in order as I had started to do? What the hell was going on?

Many long weeks later, one Dr Wotherspoon (the dramatis personae had charming names) apologised for the delay and reported that the slides, having been passed round and been the subject of discussion at many clinical meetings at different hospitals, had finally been shown to a world expert in haematopathology at University College London Hospital. Despite the 'scanty material' (surely not another needle biopsy!) provided, this expert favoured the diagnosis *not* of lung cancer but of 'follicular lymphoma', which a further investigation, this time a bone-marrow biopsy, might help to confirm. Going with the flow, I resigned myself to the fact that my condition had entered the world of semantics and that the ordeal would not be over, and my world restored to rights, until the 'fat lady sings'. The 'fat lady', in my case, turned out to be not a fat lady at all but Professor Andrew Lister, the doyen of onco-haematologists, of St Bartholomew's Hospital, London.

3

Cancer Ward

*Pavel Nikolayevich Rusanov had never been and could never
be a superstitious person but his heart sank when they wrote
'Wing 13' down on his admission card.*

ALEXANDER SOLZHENITSYN, *CANCER WARD*

Follicular lymphoma is a cancer of the immune system or
lymphocytes (a type of white blood cell) that moves around
the body. All things being equal, it is preferable to cancer
of the lung and the treatment depends upon how far the
disease has progressed. The severity of the condition is hard
to ascertain. There are many factors to consider and the lymphoma is morphologically scored from grade 1 (indolent)
to grade 3b (aggressive). There is little consensus regarding
the treatment or prognosis and the five-year survival rate
ranges from twenty to ninety-five per cent, depending on
the lymphoma type, stage, age of the patient and other vari-
ables. This variation in outlook makes a definite prognosis
extremely difficult but, as I was to learn, it can be anything
from less than one year to twenty years.

When Professor Lister agreed to take on my case I felt that
I had the best possible chances of survival and that I was in
safe hands. The Thursday haemo-oncology outpatient clinic

at 'Barts' (as St Bartholomew's Hospital, Smithfield, is affectionately known), where I was to see him, is, paradoxically, a haven of hopefulness. While all those waiting, in the serried ranks of chairs, to see the five doctors, their names, together with the numbers of their consulting rooms, scrawled in red on a wipeable board, had carcinomas to which sooner or later – some patently sooner – were going to succumb, there was, and is, the same aura of calm and optimism which, as I was later to learn, pervades the entire institution. I have been in many hospitals before and since, yet nowhere do the personnel, from the consultants to the cleaners, treat the patients with anything but the courtesy and respect that inspires confidence in an often scary situation.

My first encounter with Professor Lister was not propitious. I had yet to know him. Emerging puck-like from consulting room number 5 in his white coat and signature bow tie (a charmingly old-fashioned touch), he surveyed the lines of those waiting and casting a stern eye over them bellowed, 'Mrs Potter!' When no one moved but looked shiftily at one another, he waited a few moments before turning to go back into his room. At the same moment, a lady carrying a polystyrene mug of coffee appeared from the adjacent cafeteria. Catching sight of her, Professor Lister called out irascibly, 'Too late! Come back in three months.' How unfair, I thought, my opinion of the National Health Service going rapidly down. The next moment Mrs Potter was following the jovial Professor into his consulting room and the waiting patients, enjoying the morning's entertainment, were smiling. Over the years I was to get to know Professor Lister's quirky sense of humour, which often lightened a grim situation.

With my medical history meticulously noted with a

fountain pen, in the Professor's minuscule hand, the first page of what was to become a very thick file, was filled. Neither the diagnosis, nor the prognosis, was yet clear. The Professor's (later to become Andrew) mind was still open. There were many investigative hurdles to clear and the jury was still out. I was directed to the Bodley Scott (named after Sir Ronald Bodley Scott, a renowned oncologist) ward, where I was to be introduced to the delights of yet another biopsy, as unpleasant as the last, this time of the bone marrow.

Bodley Scott, the day ward of the oncology department, was by no stretch of the imagination Pavel Nikolyevich's depressing 'wing 13', the cancer ward with its 'cement floor … peeling paint … impersonal treatment … and spittoons which had not been cleaned'. I could not have been more warmly and courteously greeted, more encouraged to feel at ease. The Head Nurse, Filippo (later to greet me, as he did all his patients, with a kiss on each cheek and a warm hug), welcomed me by my first name and ushered me to a seat by the water cooler between a very bald young man in trainers, and a girl wearing a colourful bandanna, to hide what I guessed was her shaven head, beneath which she had defiantly hung gold hoop earrings. Moving up to make more room – the ward was pretty full – they both smiled at me and I wondered if they envied what had always been my pride and joy, my thick mass of curls, which before long would be removed to form an auburn carpet on the bathroom floor.

In the day ward, which was flooded with sunlight, everyone seemed to know each other. The half-dozen nurses in their navy-blue uniforms and name badges, and their trolleys of instruments with which I was to become familiar, extracted blood samples and administered chemotherapy to patients seated in armchairs, who would be there all day, with a chat and a smile for everyone. It was a close-knit family and any reservations I may have had, when I came out of the lift and stepped over the threshold of what was to become my second home, quickly disappeared.

It was to be a long haul and the bone-marrow biopsy was only the start. I had no idea what 'bone marrow' was, nor where it was to be found other than on a butcher's counter. I was soon to find out. After a few weeks of CAT scans, MRI scans, more X-rays and blood tests in which it seemed one's lifeblood was being drained, the big moment, which was later to fade into insignificance compared with the treats in store, arrived.

A bone-marrow biopsy, for cancers that are most likely to affect the bone marrow such as non-Hodgkin's lymphoma, my alternative diagnosis, consists in removing a one- to two-centimetre core of bone marrow (in my case from the hip bone) in one piece with a 'trephine' (a form of thick, sharp needle) at the same time as sucking up some of the cells into a syringe in order to examine them under the microscope.

The procedure was carried out by a beautiful Spanish doctor – few of the medical staff on the ward were English and, indeed, several seemed barely able to speak the language, which appeared to have little effect on their expertise – whose dark eyes were mute with sympathy for the discomfort she was inflicting behind the closed curtains of one of the cubicles in the ward. That I kicked up a bit of a dust as the trephine was inserted into the bone, while a nurse held my hand, was par for the course. The flip side was that the procedure was soon over and my long and 'happy' relationship with Bodley Scott Day Ward had begun.

Thomas Paynell, in 1528, described cancer as '… a melancholy impostume eatynge partes of the body' and the earliest definition of the term is 'a growth, lump or protuberance'. The word itself comes from the Greek *karkínos* and the Latin *cancer*, both of which mean crab (the appearance of an external tumour's swollen veins resembles a crab's legs). Cancer, unlike the equally emotive TB, was not imagined to be an aphrodisiac conferring on the patient extraordinary powers of seduction, but was thought, on the contrary, to cripple vitality and deaden desire. 'The Crab loves people. Once he's grabbed you with his pincers, he won't let you go till you croak.' Although in my case he granted me a reprieve.

I was finally diagnosed as having, not cancer of the lung but indolent, or low-grade follicular lymphoma of the lung (non-Hodgkin's lymphoma or NHL), for which the treatment of choice, as explained to me by the Professor, was to 'watch and wait'.

Attendances at the hospital became a major part of my life as I underwent, on a regular basis, a programme of X-rays, CT scans and blood tests, the latter carried out by a research phlebotomist whom Professor Lister referred to affectionately as his 'little bleeder'. The reprieve, in the event, was short-lived. Some months later a persistent cough, which developed while I was on holiday in Lake Garda and which I put down to the aftermath of a cold, took me back to the hospital where as a result of a routine scan I was hastily directed to the sanctum sanctorum, where I was informed by Professor Lister that the cancer had become 'high-grade' or aggressive, that he wanted to see me again a few days later and that this time I was to bring my husband. Everything that had gone before now faded into insignificance and I waited for the big day with apprehension.

The Professor was as serious as I had seen him. At a meeting attended by my husband and myself, his registrar and Head Nurse Filippo, he gave his 'kill or cure' verdict. The chemotherapy in its most powerful form on offer – six bouts of Chop-R, the side effects of which many patients were unable to tolerate – would, it was hoped, shrink the lesion in my lung, which had now increased considerably in size, but it had, at the same time, the potential to kill me. The choice was mine – ours – and with what seemed to be very little we opted, tearfully in my case, for what was to turn out to be the barbarous treatment. As I left the hospital having agreed to embark on what would turn out to be an exceedingly rocky road, I felt the doors of my past life slam shut behind me.

While the term 'chemotherapy' was by no means uncommon, I, like most people, had absolutely no idea of what it actually entailed. My worst fear was that I might lose my hair. It was Filippo who told me, as gently as he could, that I would. I did not believe him. Looking around at the other patients on Bodley Scott ward with their inventive headscarves and their cunning wigs, I knew that I would be different. I was not.

The nightmare, like most nightmares, has no chronological sequence but has transmuted into a journey through Hades in which, for what seemed a very long time indeed, no light was visible at the end of the tunnel.

Chemotherapy, in its most general sense, refers to treatment of disease by chemicals that kill cells. These 'chemotherapeutic' drugs work by impairing cell division and effectively target fast-dividing cells. Unfortunately, scientists have yet to identify specific features of malignant cells that would make them uniquely targetable. This means that other fast-dividing cells, such as those responsible for hair growth and replacement of the stomach lining, are also affected by the treatment. If the dose of these potentially fatal chemicals is too low, it will be ineffective against the tumour, if it is too high it will be intolerable to the patient. The dose is adjusted for the 'body surface area', calculated with a mathematical formula using the patient's weight and height, and correlates with blood volume. A cocktail of these potentially lethal drugs is administered intravenously and under strict supervision. While a too high dose would prove fatal to the patient, even the most tailor-made dose will be physically exhausting and carries a high risk of side effects the long list of which includes pain, anaemia, fever, weakness, muscle aches, dizziness, headache, skin rash, itching, swelling of the tongue and throat, low blood pressure, haemorrhage, heart, liver and kidney problems, potentially lethal infections and sepsis (due to depression of the immune system), nausea, vomiting and the dreaded hair loss that I was determined, at all costs, to avoid.

In order to counter these potential 'treats', a potpourri of other drugs, each with its own side effect, was prescribed to minimise those precipitated by the treatment itself. To say that from the first day that I presented myself in Bodley Scott as a chemotherapy patient my life was put on hold was an understatement. Fortunately, although the principles of the treatment had been explained to me, I had little idea what to expect.

There is treatment before you start the treatment. Not only the weighing and the measuring of body mass but the blood tests, during which several glass phials were filled, which were sent by messenger to the lab to be analysed. If the results of the blood test were satisfactory, the pharmacy would prepare your individual chalice of drugs which, after several weary and apprehensive hours of waiting, would be delivered to the ward.

Having swallowed an assortment of steroid and other pills to prevent sickness and any allergic reactions, a thin, flexible tube was inserted into a vein (if the nurse could find a suitable one) in your hand or arm, after which the potentially harmful drugs with deceptively poetic names such as rituximab, vincristine and cyclophosphamide, to name but three, were delivered via the cannula into your bloodstream. Although later, if all went well, I was to graduate to an armchair in the exclusive area of other patients receiving chemotherapy, the first treatment was administered unbelievably slowly by the Head Nurse himself over four incredibly patient and watchful hours as I lay on the bed in a cubicle. When the long day was over, you were sent home to recover with a 'party bag' of drugs, which had to be ingested on a daily basis and which came with a complicated list of instructions one of which was to take your temperature each day and to contact the ward if you became even slightly unwell. Filippo and his angelic staff did not wait for you to do this but telephoned frequently to enquire, as if they really cared, exactly how you were feeling. Although I realise that Barts may be a special case, anyone who says a word against the National Health Service will get a piece of my mind.

I will draw a veil over the next few months of scans, blood counts and week-long admissions to our local hospital – the emergency ambulance was not permitted to take me as far as Barts – during which I became not only a zombie, scarcely able to think, talk, or walk without holding on to the walls, but a Bodley Scott habitué, a member of an elite and cohesive club. Suffice it to say that any pretensions to normal life were put on hold as one struggled to cope with pain and exhaustion, insomnia, restless limbs and stomach cramps, kidney and bladder infections, nausea, loss of appetite and weight. When my white cell count fell alarmingly and I could tolerate the killer regime no longer and despite my protests that I would carry on in the interests of defeating the cancer, the treatment was discontinued and the remains of the tumour targeted with radiotherapy.

I haven't mentioned my hair. I lost it, of course, together with my eyelashes and eyebrows. The trauma is indescribable and with the best intention in the world and despite the knowledge that personal vanity is low on the scale of a life-threatening illness, I wept copiously when the loose remaining tufts of what I had always considered to be a very important part of my appearance were removed. Who was this skeleton in the mirror? Where had my old persona, the one I was used to, gone? The sight of my bald head and people's reaction to it was not only a constant reminder that I had cancer but made me feel vulnerable and exposed. Advised to do so by the hospital before I had lost my hair, I had already bought my wig. In the specialist wig shop the staff were patient and understanding and, in no mood to avail myself of the opportunity of trying a completely different hairstyle or colour, I chose a curly model as close to my own hair as I could get. Pulling it on, I looked at myself in the mirror, I rather liked it. In the event I grew to hate it. I had never worn a hat, I disliked the feel of anything on my head, and this monstrosity was worse. It was ugly – nobody could mistake it for real hair with its shiny and artificial diffusion of light – and it was hot. I took to wearing turbans or headscarves in a variety of colours and materials or, despite the sensation of a chill wind on one's sensitive scalp, nothing at all on my head – scaring the postman and the grandchildren – round the house.

When measured against the chemotherapy, the radiotherapy was a doddle, notwithstanding the fact that one was permanently branded, in three places on the neck and chest, with the indelible mark of Cain. Again there were side effects and strictures (kill or cure) and lotions and potions to be applied. Lying naked from the waist up in the radiotherapy department on the trolley while a million milliwatts of lethal rays were directed at the tumour, hoping to finish it off, was cold and uncomfortable but not too unpleasant. Again the radiographers were charming and helpful. After each treatment I crossed the courtyard of the hospital to visit my friends in Bodley Scott. I remained a frequent visitor to the ward until the tumour was seen to shrink in size and it was felt that the mighty armoury of David had conquered the cancer of Goliath and I was declared to be in remission. How long this would last was anybody's guess. Gradually my sessions with the Professor became less frequent and the intervals between the check-ups longer.

As my winter of discontent gave way to spring I began to put on some of the weight I had lost and my hair, at first in wisps soft as a baby's, began to grow. It was hardly surprising that the colour of the new growth was not my habitual reddish-brown, which owed its youthful tints to Jo Hansford in her Mount Street salon and which cost a king's ransom to maintain. I made the decision to succumb to nature and to take the money saved. Although I still have difficulty in recognising the woman who stares back at me from the looking-glass and although the regrowth was not quick – nature takes its time – I now have a head of not unattractive silver curls appropriate to my age.

As of today, the lymphoma is still in remission. My appointments with Andrew Lister take place at ever-increasing intervals and, after a brief examination to detect any 'lumps the size of golf balls' in my neck or groin, consist largely of talk not of my cancer, which is rapidly dealt with, but of the theatre. Andrew's son Tom is a playwright with a current production at the Edinburgh Festival, and I am shortly to have my third play *An Eligible Man* produced.

Looking back on my *annus horribilis*, I experienced not only the almost embarrassing kindness of comparative strangers as they put themselves at my disposal and showered me with good deeds and appropriate small gifts, but the support of my close family who demonstrated feelings that came as a humbling surprise to me and which had never been fully displayed. While I relied on the unfailing and uncomplaining support and encouragement of my husband, in my four daughters I discovered four Jewish mothers as they fussed and fretted over me, visited constantly, accompanied me to hospital visits and kept my refrigerator filled with food, which for much of the time I was unable to eat.

Now that it's all over I can concentrate on happier things. While I have less confidence than previously in my immortality, it does not occur to me to ask, 'Why me?' Why not me? In Bodley Scott I met patients, half, a quarter of my age, young men and women with their lives before them (luckily it was not a children's ward). If I were to question what I had done to deserve the visitation from the Crab, the answer would be 'nothing'. I am only experiencing what it is to be human. I do not regard the disease as the 'supernatural punishment' of the *Iliad* and the *Odyssey*, neither am I a cancerophobe, like Norman Mailer, who got rid of the 'repressed feelings' (thought responsible for the disease) by stabbing his wife in the mistaken belief that had he not killed her he would have 'gotten cancer and been dead in a few years himself'. I refuse to be a 'victim'. I do not believe that Nature is taking her revenge on a wicked technocratic world, and I will not endow my illness with some atavistic 'meaning' that takes no account of the random malignant gene for which, somewhere along the line, I have been singled out.

4

Dead Letter Perfect

Comedy is an essential part of playmaking.

ALAN AYCKBOURN

My third stage play *An Eligible Man* was adapted from my novel of the same name, which had been published twenty years earlier. The novel's first reincarnation was a commissioned six-part series for London Weekend Television. This was scrapped at the vital moment by the commissioning editor, Nick Elliott, who defected to the BBC and – despite the fact that he had approved the scripts and paid me for them – was unable to take the series with him. For the writer, who has expended a very great deal of time and energy on the adaptation of her novel, while very disappointing this is par for the course. My first undertaking, after I had seen off the Crab for what I hoped was a very long time, was once again to rewrite *An Eligible Man,* this time as a stage play. This was a medium in which, not least for the moment when the play is firing on all cylinders and you have the audience eating out of your hand, I was getting increasingly interested.

With the West End theatres full of fail-safe revivals, musicals and stage versions of classic films, and off-West End and fringe theatres strapped for cash, I knew that the prospects for getting a play produced were exceedingly gloomy if not worse. Impelled, however, by the unfathomable optimism that drives all writers when they embark on a new piece of work, I began to transpose my novel, which had sold well and attracted good reviews.

To date, as far as stage work was concerned, my very first play *Home Truths* (starring the late Christopher Cazenove and Edward Hardwicke) had had a successful four-and-a-half-month tour at number one venues in the regions (including the Churchill Theatre, Bromley, and the Yvonne Arnaud Theatre, Guildford, which had co-produced it) and my second, *Change of Heart* (on which I based my novel *Intensive Care*), had played for six weeks at the New End Theatre, Hampstead. While not superstitious and with little interest in the occult, it did occur to me to wonder whether this last, which was about the longest survivor of a heart-lung transplant, had had any bearing on my own lung problems, which became manifest on the last night of the run. I don't think so. But somewhere, the play and the problem formed a macabre connection in the further reaches of my mind.

I was under no illusions. In a culture obsessed with celebrity, I was aware that the 'well-made' or 'straight' play, unless it could attract at least one theatrical 'star' or one from a popular TV soap, was a doomed species. Nonetheless I was weary of writing novels and had recently walked out of too many bad plays at half-time because I had no interest at all in staying till the end. Agreeing, in essence, with Dominic Cooke, the artistic director of the Royal Court – 'There have been too many plays about outsiders and the dispossessed on our stages and not enough about the middle classes, who

after all, make up the bulk of our theatre-going population'
– I set to work.

While many playwrights strive to live up to Shakespeare,
my own role model was Alan Ayckbourn, that purveyor of
laughter to the middle classes and twice as prolific as Shakespeare, from whom I learned, among many other things,
that comedy is an essential part of playmaking (without light
how can we possibly create shadow?), that an audience needs
to 'care' about your characters and that the English language,
while a nightmare of imprecision for law-makers, is a God-
given present of double-entendres for the dramatist.

I did not look at the novel. Novel writing and playwriting
are two very different kettles of fish. In the novel the narrative gives you freedom not only to have as many characters
as you like and to spell out their trajectories at length, but
to take them wheresoever you please and inject your own
comments and opinions into the text. In the stage play the
number of characters in the cast is strictly limited (every
actor costs the theatre money, and money is what theatres
have little of), they are grounded for two hours on the stage,
and the only 'journeys' they can make are the changes they
undergo during the course of the play. Few of us remain the
same. Although in real life these changes take place over
the years, it is good to allow the audience to witness character changes taking place on stage as a result of events. It is
important to have some sort of map in your head on which
you can plot exactly where your characters are going, and
no actor should be the same person when the 'curtain' –
metaphorical these days – goes down as he was when it went
up. These emotional (and sometimes physical) changes are
brought about both through the action and the dialogue,
which must be as concise as possible.

At the beginning of the drama the character has no history within the context of the play. He may have a previous history that unfolds as the story is told, but with his initial appearance he has only a present and a future as far as the plot is concerned. 'Exposition' is simply the presentation of material an audience needs to know. Each 'backstory' – the characters' circumstances such as their names, jobs and relationships to the others in the play – is new to the world in which it exists. Unlike the novelist, the playwright cannot go back in time and fill in the details but must find other ways of getting the information across. This does not mean that an actor has to make long-winded speeches to let the audience know who he is, his current situation, or where he has sprung from. Information gleaned indirectly by an audience is far more effective and, if it is important, it should be conveyed at least twice. Greetings such as 'My old friend Patrick!' or 'The last time I saw you, Sally, was at that architects' meeting,' props such as a pile of legal books, or a 'badge of office' such as an apron or white coat, are some of the strategies in the playwright's armoury. The exposition does not have to come at the beginning of the play, nor does it have to be revealed all at once. The information can be eked out over time and the golden rule of both film and stage is 'show, don't tell'. You can sometimes learn as much about a character over a coffee or a beer as you can from knowing him/her for several years: provided you know, or are subtly told, what to look for. What the characters *don't say*, or when they don't answer the question that is being asked of them, can be every bit as revealing as what they do say.

Another practical way of conveying information is through the 'set' which, before a word is spoken, can indicate the period during which the play is taking place as well as something about the taste and financial status of its inhabitants. At the opening of each scene there may be changes – the remnants of a meal or some empty bottles and glasses – which will indicate that time has passed.

The mark of a good script is its stage directions, which should impart only essential information and be kept to the minimum. Bracketed instructions – (furiously), (haughtily), (passionately) – before a character gets to speak are anathema to the actor to whom no space is given: they are the mark of an amateur. Good actors can say a lot with their faces and body language, and space must be left for them to do so. The smallest gesture can speak volumes and replace pages of text.

Holding the attention of the audience – which should never be underestimated, they pick up on much more than you think – for two hours is probably the hardest challenge of all. If you have done your job properly, they should not need to read the programme (usually a waste of money unless you want to study it later at home) to sort out who is who. A good story and strong characters – together with a subplot or 'B' story – will help, but other weapons are variety, suspense and tension, which the writer will sense rather than manipulate. As in music, the pace and mood must change, *allegro* must be followed by *adagio, animato* by *andante*, otherwise you will have committed the worst crime of all: you will bore your audience.

Where does one start?

Advised by my then theatrical agent, Micheline Steinberg, to seek the help of a 'dramaturg', and wanting *An Eligible Man* to be a success, I took her advice.

'Dramaturgy' is the art of dramatic composition and

many writers work with a specialist, or dramaturg, when adapting a work for the stage. It was Aristotle, around 350 BC, observing the writers of his time, who first used the appellation. Regarding drama as a subsection of poetry, he analysed the relations between character and action, speech and story, gave examples of plots and examined the reaction that the plays awoke in the audience. Many of his 'rules' are associated with the *deus ex machina,* an improbable contrivance or sudden unexpected solution to an intractable problem, which is brought in by the playwright at the last moment. The term *deus ex machina* or 'god from the machine' refers to the conventions of Greek tragedy, where a *mechane* or crane was used to lower actors, playing a god or gods, on to the stage. Sometimes they were brought up by risers through a trapdoor.

The Greek tragedian, Euripides, was particularly fond of this device and was criticised by Aristotle (*Poetics*) who argued that the resolution of a plot must arise internally and must follow from some previous action in the play. Critical of the irrational element in Sophocles' *Oedipus* he states: '... the unravelling of the plot, no less than the complication, must arise out of the plot itself, it must not be brought about by the *deus ex machina* ...' For the writer, the use of this device generally implies a lack of skill because it takes no account of the story's internal logic and it is often so unlikely that it challenges Coleridge's famous 'suspension of disbelief'.

In the UK dramaturgs are often playwrights, sometimes manqué, themselves. They help dramatists to learn their craft and develop their scripts. Previously having written mainly fiction, having had only two plays produced and always willing to learn, I thought that the services of a dramaturg might help me hone my skills.

For what seemed a very long time, under the watchful eye of my dramaturg, I was not allowed to write my play. I had first to choose my characters (in the case of *An Eligible Man* six of them) and then to write down their stories, dissect their personalities and spell out where they were coming from, what they wanted and where they were going. It took me a long time and I felt as if I were back at school. Having established the dramatis personae, I then had to examine the 'plot'. A step outline – a great many versions were required – was drafted, giving a breakdown of what happened in each 'scene' and the sequence of events. When the final step outline had been approved, I had to provide a detailed scene-by-scene and moment-by-moment synopsis of the action, which was followed by a 'treatment'. Not until I had completed all these exercises was I allowed to start on the play itself, by which time I was thoroughly confused and jaded. Shakespeare, I would bet my bottom dollar, had never laboriously penned Hamlet's backstory, nor written a dozen or more step outlines before he embarked upon *Othello*. I doubt if Beethoven indulged in a programme of five-finger exercises before composing his orchestral works. All I needed to rely on was the classical basics: the unities of place, time and setting. I dismissed the dramaturg, breathed a sigh of relief, and started to write my play.

As with novels, the playwright 'knows because he knows'. All the dramaturgs in the world notwithstanding, there is no more to the creative process than that. It is the answer one cannot give, it sounds so unhelpful, when one is asked how one writes. With plays it is a gut feeling. If you don't like your characters neither will the audience; when you are bored so will they be; as you move them around on the stage like chess pieces, you inhabit their skins; you are the ventriloquist and they your dummies. If the piece is to come alive you must live it. Some dramatists read their work aloud, for me there is no need, I hear their distinct voices, *fortissimo* sometimes, in my head. With my new easy-to-use American scriptwriting program Final Draft, comes a facility: at the press of a button a flat and robotic voice in your computer, playing the parts of all your characters, reads your play aloud. I find this amusing but unhelpful. For the time that she takes to write it the author *is* the play: she is both the men and the women, the old and the young, the weak and the strong, the comic and the tragic. It is very exhausting but infinitely satisfying; like nothing else in the world.

The first draft is the first draft. One sees one's mistakes. There will be many others. One refines and refines, fully rounded characters take time to evolve and one injects into each of them not only shards of one's own personality but scraps of everyone one has ever known as one moves them, like chess pieces, around a mental stage. How the characters relate to the writer is of no consequence, what is important is how they relate to each other.

There are practical elements to consider. How can your protagonist be expected to change 'leisure wear' to 'formal evening' when you have allowed him only two minutes between scenes? Will the budget run to the excessive number of 'props' you have called for? What devices have you employed to get your characters on and off the stage? Will the elaborate set you have stipulated need the services of a top-notch (expensive) designer? Are so many actors called for that the play, as far as producers are concerned, is a non-starter? Have you included so many 'sound effects'

– mobile phones, doorbells and slams, incidental music – that the stage manager will have her work cut out?

One mustn't underestimate the importance of the 'off-stage' character. As with props, they add a third dimension, a feeling that there is a world outside the stage. Invisible spirits can hover over the proceedings and reinforce what could well have turned out to be stock or stereotypical characters had they actually appeared. Depending on one's skill as a writer, these external figures can affect the drama as successfully as the on-stage actors and must be considered, and written, equally carefully. By talking about, or referring to, relatives or friends whom the audience will never see, your dramatis personae will give your off-stage characters life. Audiences are to be entertained, full stop. Dramatists must reject all characterisation, explanation and emotional history for plots that ensure we long to know what happens next. His/her job, after all, is to keep 'bums on seats'.

An Eligible Man is a 'comedy of grief' which, for its stage version, was inspired by Mark Twain: 'Humour is the effort to throw off, to fight back the burden of grief that is laid on each one of us.' In the play a widowed and grieving circuit judge finds himself pursued by three very different women. One seduces him, one offers intellectual companionship and one introduces him to her glamorous social life. With which one of them will he find the happiness he has lost and the contentment he is seeking? In the best plays (and films for that matter) the protagonist has to 'want' something. His Honour Judge Christopher Osgood in *An Eligible Man* was no exception. Whether he gets it, or whether he does not, marks the difference between comedy and tragedy. A comedy has been defined as a play in which someone wants something and eventually gets what he wants (after a considerable journey), and tragedy as a play where he doesn't. Neither of these options says more or less about the human condition. They just say it in different ways.

Typing the title of the play (with 'First Draft' and the date at the top of the page), followed by the cast list together with their ages and brief description ('A circuit judge', 'A novelist', 'A fashion-buyer'), and a paragraph about the set and where the action was taking place, I was on my way.

A first draft is a first draft. Eventually the number of the drafts could be counted in double figures. At least. *An Eligible Man* was no exception. Plays are organic and will not only be altered and refined by the author, but later (unless you are Harold Pinter) by the director, who will bring his/ her own ideas to it (about which more later) and by the actors who will have theirs. Writing a play is all very well. What was needed now was a producer who would put his money where his mouth was and breathe life into it.

Pleased with my script about which I was very excited, I sent it to Micheline Steinberg who kept it for several weeks. When I called her she told me that she didn't think the play was going to work and that she couldn't really get behind it. Disappointed after waiting such a long time for her reaction, I took the play back, dusted myself down, and set about finding a theatre for it. I was on my own.

5

The Casting Couch

The play's the thing ...

WILLIAM SHAKESPEARE

All I had to do was find a theatre. Easier said than done. The West End was an impossible place to crack. Much of the audience for straight plays was already well-served by subsidised venues – such as the Royal National Theatre – while in the regions ninety per cent of the audience were over fifty with the matinees attended by elderly people who did not like going out at night. This did not bode well for the future. Again the demand for celebrities came into play. Two of Jonathan Miller's recent productions, *Hamlet* in Bristol and *The Cherry Orchard* in Sheffield, were unable, despite rave reviews, to find a West End producer because his excellent cast (to whom he remained loyal) included no 'famous' names. Stardom, rather than direction, is as important to a serious understanding of the theatre as it is to the movies. *Grand Hotel* is not an Edmund Goulding but a Greta Garbo picture, and no one rushed to see *The Philadelphia Story* because George Cukor had directed it but because Cary Grant, Katharine Hepburn and James Stewart starred in it; Humphrey Bogart *is* the Maltese Falcon.

Without a star from television or film willing to commit to a long run, the advice to playwrights, as far as West End theatre is concerned is 'don't even think about it!' I didn't.

At intervals, and having taken the precaution to speak first to the artistic directors of the various theatres where I thought there might be a chance of getting my play produced and who were willing to read it, I sent the script to the Palace Theatre, Watford, the Churchill Theatre, Bromley (where my first play had been produced), the Orange Tree Theatre, Richmond, and the Finborough Theatre among several others. Artistic directors are notoriously as overworked as their theatres are strapped for cash. Their desks are piled high with scripts and, the track record of the author notwithstanding, they will take anything from three to nine months to read them. If, indeed, they get round to reading them at all. Tactful enquiries at suitable intervals as to exactly where your precious baby was in the pipeline brought back inventive responses such as 'our artistic director is leaving and her replacement won't be taking over for a few weeks', 'your script has gone to a panel of readers and the process will take at least six months', 'our theatre is fully committed for the next two years' and 'what did you say the name of your play was? We'll look into the correspondence and chase it up.'

While all this was taking place I was encouraged by several people whose opinion I valued. Robert Young, a veteran and respected director who had read the script, called me from Los Angeles in the small hours to tell me he 'thought it wonderful' and although he was fully committed to film at the present time he looked forward to directing it at a future date. 'A fine piece of work, sparkling dialogue, terrific characters and also very funny' – this from a well-known actor. 'Stylish, intelligent, literate, fun, well written, has good roles and is commercial' – from a renowned agent who unfortunately was about to retire. 'I enjoyed *An Eligible Man*. The writing is strong and the characters are too' – from the head of development at a radio production company.

It wasn't, however, until I sent the script to the New End, Hampstead, where my previous play *Change of Heart* had been staged, that I received a positive response from a theatre.

The artistic director of the New End, Ninon Jerome, liked *An Eligible Man* and asked me to come to the theatre to discuss it. Hallelujah. There was a chance that my play might be produced. From then on, until that moment of indescribable moments, the first night, it was (reasonably) plain sailing. Ninon and I got on like a house on fire and after several meetings over cups of coffee in Hampstead to discuss possible time slots and casting, we were on our way. Casting for off-West End theatre, as well as for West End theatre itself, is of the essence, both for artistic integrity and the financial success of the play. We made ambitious lists of 'names' from stage and television. Even if the response to the script was positive ('good luck with the play') they were either far too busy or unable to commit themselves to a six-week run in Hampstead (suppose Steven Spielberg called them at the crucial moment?). One well-known and definitely 'box office actor' (who shall be nameless) to whom we offered the eponymous title role took three months to make up his mind during which we were bound by professional etiquette not to offer it to another actor. When the answer came it was ambiguous: 'Yes, he loved it but *thought* he was going to Australia. Could it wait another year?' Could it hell. The play had been scheduled for a spring production and the slot was not negotiable. How long does it take to read a script? Although we were by no means scraping the bottom of the barrel, our list of possible names was shrinking rapidly. Ninon, a delightful optimist, was not dismayed however, and auditions for the leading man and for the five other members of the cast were put in place.

Casting, like most other exercises in the theatre, is a catch 22 situation. An actor who is well-known will attract other well-known actors: an unknown leading man (no matter how talented an actor) will make the supporting cast nervous as to the play's success and the possibility of getting it reviewed. Ninon's list of 'possibles', some of whom she had known and had worked with, and many of whom came straight out of *Spotlight*, was long. We set to work.

Casting a play is not only a matter of talent and availability but of personality. However suitable an actor, he/she has to be someone the director will be able to work with for however long it takes. A pain in the neck is a pain in the neck. Arriving late and dishevelled for the audition, no matter what the excuse, being unnecessarily pushy or argumentative or failing to read the script if he/she has been sent it, will not endear him/her to the director. If the script has not been sent in advance, the hopefuls will have been given the appropriate few pages to look at in the allotted ten minutes before they are called to audition.

It is never easy. Despite the fact that the number of people applying to drama schools and acting courses has reached unprecedented levels and is going up every year, it is twice as difficult to get into drama school as it is to Oxbridge. Although there were more than 800 applicants for the six parts on offer in *An Eligible Man*, finding 'quality' actors, all waiting desperately to be 'spotted', is like searching for the proverbial needle in the theatrical haystack.

The auditions took place for the most part in the comfortable bar, with its stage-pink velvet-covered sofas, of the New End Theatre. Having puffed their way up the Hampstead hill, the applicants who had been weeded out from the long list of hopefuls, waited downstairs in the foyer until their names were called. This gave us time not only to audition the previous actor but to bone up on CVs (printouts from *Spotlight*, the actors' bible) with which we were provided. These printouts, furnished with photographs (often time-expired and air-brushed) of each applicant, gave us not only information of his/her physical appearance – height, weight, hair and eye colour – but such details as 'role types' (white, Eastern European), voice character, voice quality and playing age, the latter frequently adjusted downwards. A list of acting credits, stage, TV, film and radio, together with appropriate dates, was followed by 'accents and dialects' (American-Standard, Australian, cockney, Northern, Received Pronunciation, Yorkshire), 'music and dance' (ballad, blues, cabaret and jazz), 'skills' (animal-handling, snooker, lacrosse, stage-combat), and 'languages' (English, Gaelic, French, Spanish, Cantonese, Mandarin).

Auditioning is hard work. Often Ninon's list had more than fifty names on it and these were called at ten-minute intervals. Sometimes we had only a fifteen-minute – if any – respite for lunch. Dedicated theatre people not only work long hours but seem to live on air. They are bothered neither about time nor food, which is partaken of not at regular but (in)convenient moments. During the two gruelling weeks of auditions in which you are so immersed both mentally and physically you can forget not only about the outside world but about exercise and fresh air; I took care to get plenty of sleep and to have surreptitious sandwiches and a bag of Werther's Original butter candies in my bag.

The casting process is both fascinating and formulaic. Two chairs are set up on one of which sits a 'reader' (a member of the theatre staff and often an aspiring actor) who will painstakingly and tirelessly give the actors their 'feed', repeating the same lines with equal enthusiasm time after time, so that they can read their prospective parts either from the script or from the printed 'sides' they have been given.

Very often a lot can be gauged about the aspirants as soon as they walk through the door. They are confident and calm or bedraggled – as if they have just rolled out of bed – and harassed having set out too late for the audition. They will look you in the eye and hold out their hands confidently to be shaken or mutter and mumble as they sidle into the waiting chair. Ninon was never fazed by their behaviour. The best of actors could be nervous and the worst confident. As far as she was concerned the playing field was level and everyone had an equal chance. By the end of the day I wondered why many of them had given up their day jobs and could see that as far as the stage was concerned not only would they never be 'spotted' but that they hadn't a hope in hell.

Actors, however, are a deluded bunch. They live their dreams. There was not one who did not think that on the strength of the audition he/she would qualify at worst for a recall, even if not the part. Some of them were dire. Many of them just didn't get what was required from them, even though Ninon assiduously gave them a potted version of the background to the scene they were doing and some idea of the character they were to play. No matter how dreadful their performance, however, no matter how inappropriate their initial reading or how bad their interpretation of the script, she always gave them a second chance. 'Well done,' she'd say at the end of each rendition, then she'd explain a little more about what they were supposed to be doing and invite them to 'give it another go'. And they did. And they were no better. But at least they went away with their dignity intact and feeling that the journey to Hampstead from sometimes quite distant parts of the country had been worth it and that they had not been rejected out of hand.

There was a big difference in approach. The happy-go-lucky ones who drove a coach and horses through their lines and would never make it past a Christmas pantomime gave precisely the same performance – despite having been given helpful notes by the director – the second time round; the dull ones were dull and the eager incomprehensible, while some were so totally unsuited to the part they were auditioning for, you wondered why their agents had sent them and why they had bothered to audition at all. Those who had done their homework and brought some measure of intelligence to the proceedings stood out. Having asked if we minded them asking a few questions and eager to get a psychological fix on the character they were hoping to play, they enquired not only about his/her backstory but his/her relationship to the other actors. We sat up and took notice and an immediate telephone call to the appropriate agent secured a recall for his/her client. We were generally in agreement. The wheat stood out from the chaff. To a man they went away hopefully, shaking our hands, and saying 'thank you' for the opportunity and how nice it had been to meet us. Sometimes they forgot their umbrellas or their briefcases and came scurrying back; sometimes they reappeared uninvited and begged for another chance. None of them, however unsuitable, went home humiliated. As a result of Ninon's good nature and her patience, even at the end of a long and exhausting day, they left with their heads held high and with their *amour propre* intact. It is a cruel business. Most of them were out of work and some of them looked as if they were starving, if not for want of food for want of employment. It was a choice, thankless as it appeared to be, they had made.

On the first day of auditions we were in luck. One of the female roles (three women in pursuit of the 'eligible' man, a widowed circuit judge) was the glamorous forty-year-old Lady Jo Henderson, a district judge. When the first applicant for the role, Sonia Saville, was ushered in, we could not believe our eyes. In a couture navy-blue suit and pearls, hair swept to the top of her head, a cut-glass accent, and the looks and legs of a fashion model she seemed too good to be true. But could she act? She could. And as we discovered later she was actually a lawyer in real life. An immediate call to her agent gave us our first member of the cast.

The auditions went on all day, all week … and all the following week, during which the New End Theatre was booked and we moved to the Henry Irving Studio at the Royal Academy of Dramatic Art. Finally we had a first-rate cast, which included Graham Seed (Nigel Pargeter from the long-running radio serial *The Archers*) and Patricia Potter (from TV's *Holby City*) who before very long were, as Robert Young insisted every actor should be, 'dead letter perfect'.

They were a happy family and bonded from the day of the first 'read-through' of the script to the sad moment – tears all round – when the final curtain came down. Their gratitude to me for choosing them to be in my play, about which they could not speak too highly, was touching.

Like the summer, once you have a play performed, you

never want it to end. While I sat in my playwright's seat in the back row of the theatre for almost every performance – no two of which were the same – I did not attend every rehearsal. First, they went on all day and were extremely tiring, and second, because it was not fair on the director who must be given her head. 'Rehearsals' are a comparatively modern custom. In Shakespeare's day the company may well have had no more than one group rehearsal, and many actors would have gone on stage at the first performance word-perfect but unclear as to who it was who was addressing them, whom they were supposed to address, how long they were going to have to wait between cues, and whether a short line was prose or part of a shared blank-verse line. A 'role' or roll – the rolled up set of lines or cues – was an actor's property and later actors were meant to perform it as their predecessor had done. Because of censorship, as well as the tyranny of the cue script, there seemed to be little room for innovation. When I did 'sit in' on rehearsals, it was fascinating; if I had comments to make on the performance, I knew sufficient about the fragile egos of the performers not to make them to the cast directly but to convey them to Ninon, who knew how best to handle her 'nursery' of performers.

At the end of every day the actors were given a 'call sheet' by the highly efficient stage manager, Marie Costa, in which they were formally addressed – Mr Seed, Miss Potter – told the time they would be needed the following day and advised on which scene or scenes they would be required to work on. Everyone concerned in the production also received copious daily 'rehearsal notes'. These comprised such instructions for props as 'Can Mr Seed have a pair of half-moon judge's spectacles please?'; 'A couple of cushions will be required for the sofa'; 'Is the gap between the bookshelves high enough for the wine bottle to be set on?'; 'The newspaper for Mr James should be the *Telegraph*'. Marie's job also entailed masterminding sound effects and ensuring that phones rang and music was heard at exactly the right moment. A few seconds' delay (*after* the actor had pushed the button on the radio) would not only amuse the audience, causing them to lose concentration, but discombobulate the cast. Stage manager was a responsible job and one to be taken seriously, as were those of the set designer and lighting designer (coincidentally the talented David Kydd who had worked on my first play *Home Truths*!) who could make or break a production. I was very lucky to have such a dedicated and professional team.

All good things must come to an end, however, and *An Eligible Man* was no exception. Despite minor catastrophes – the opening coincided with a production of *War and Peace* at the Hampstead Theatre, a new play at the Orange Tree, Richmond, and the RSC's Shakespeare cycle at the Round House, a heatwave during which no one wanted to come to the theatre, the road outside New End was dug up and traffic diverted, the advent of both the credit crunch and half-term – the six-week run was extremely successful. How well a play is received can often be judged by the length of time that elapses between the last spoken words and the applause. It is the same with music:

> The last sound is not the end of the music … It must be related to the silence which follows it. This is why it is so disruptive when an enthusiastic audience applauds before the final sound has died away, because there is one last moment of expressivity, which is precisely the relationship between

the end of the sound and the beginning of the silence that follows it. In this respect music is a mirror of life, because both start and end in nothing.*

The last night came too soon for both myself and the cast. We had only the evocative playbills and production shots, and for the most part extremely encouraging reviews – three stars in *The Times* and comments such as 'a touching and hilarious comedy of grief'; 'Great play, talented performers, Go see it'; and 'A civilised, amusing, intelligent entertainment' from other newspapers, the solace of glowing letters of appreciation and feedback from a happy audience – to look back on.

Had my former agent, Micheline Steinberg, been right in her reluctance to handle the piece? I don't think so. As it turned out I quickly found another agent in Nicki Stoddart (from United Agents and late of the troubled Peters, Fraser and Dunlop), who came to see *An Eligible Man.* On the strength of the writing she agreed to represent me – no small matter from an agent of her calibre whose stable includes, amongst others, Michael Frayn and Alan Bennett – and immediately sold the play, after a bidding war between two agents, to Germany.

A memorable party on our terrace on the last night (the only hot evening of the year) to which I had invited everyone involved in the play, turned out to be an emotional finale as everyone hugged everyone (as actors do), tears were shed and friendships cemented. Fraught as it was at various moments when disaster struck and everything threatened to come apart, the experience, as always as far as the theatre

---

* Daniel Barenboim

is concerned, was memorable – more exciting than a thousand novels – and one on no account to be missed.

6

Déjà Vu

Domestic misfortunes are the only serious misfortunes.
WILKIE COLLINS

We had been on holiday in Sicily, soaking up Monte Tauro with its views of the rocky coastline and the blue-green sea, revelling in the magnificent bay of Isola Bella, when disaster struck.

One of the family jokes was that each time we returned from holiday, no matter where, nor for how long we had been away, as we turned the corner of the road to wherever we happened to be living at the time, my husband would say 'I hope the house hasn't burned down!' This time it had and his irrational fears became reality. Well, not quite.

As we waited to reclaim our baggage from the carousel at Gatwick, relaxed and still in holiday mode, our mobiles rang, mine with the evocative rhythm of the Guatemalan marimba and my husband's with the more sedate 'old car horn'. Garbled and hysterical messages conveyed the news that a serious fire was blazing, not in our apartment, but in the one directly below. Thinking that we were still sunning ourselves in Taormina (in actual fact it had rained a great deal of the time) we were warned that the entire building had been evacuated and that under no circumstances were we to come home.

In a moment the Teatro Greco, gouged out of the hillside, with its curving rows of seats from which we had conjured up images of gladiatorial spectacles, the Giardino Publico, with its palm and banana trees and birds of paradise, were forgotten – it was as if they had never been – as we faced each other and tried to make sense of the news.

Our luggage took for ever to appear, the minicab we had ordered even longer and the traffic along the M23 was static. Shaken and silent, we wondered not only would we ever get home but would we find one when we got there. Had my husband's half-joking 'return from holiday' prediction, for the first time, come true?

Yes and no. By the time we arrived the fire, the flames which had, it appeared, leapt from the windows of the apartment below ours, had been extinguished, three of the half-dozen fire engines had left and the shaken residents, in various states of dress, who had been summarily evacuated from the site, were making their shocked and silent way back into the building.

Cambridge Gate, which stands at the south-east end of Regent's Park, was originally a terrace of houses built in 1875 on the site of the old Colosseum, a circular exhibition hall with a glazed cupola and a massive portico designed, not by John Nash as were the other terraces in the Park, but by Decimus Burton. The vast hall was used for exhibitions and panoramas of London, which first became unfashionable and after a time fell into desuetude. The Colosseum was demolished and replaced by ten Victorian houses, which kept to the original building line and were erected in its place. The building was designed by architects

Messrs Archer and Green and was adorned with ornate gates and lamps by ironsmith John Peachey, in the same distinctive French style as the Café Royal in Regent Street, Whitehall Court and the Hyde Park Hotel. Cambridge Gate is easily recognisable as the only stone-fronted terrace in the park. It abuts Denys Lasdun's contrasting modern and functional Royal College of Physicians with its interesting Panelled Room, which dates from before the Great Fire of 1666 and which the college has preserved. In 1997 the Cambridge Gate we know today, and which for many years had been neglected and used as offices by the Crown Estate itself, was modernised and renovated as residential properties. The interiors were refurbished as a series of flats and houses (one with swimming pool) by Cambridge Gate Development Ltd. Fortunately the architects, the Conservation Practice, not only kept the character of the property but maintained its structural integrity, which ensured that although our apartment, on the top floor of one of the original houses, was severely affected by smoke damage, it had not, as it might have been in a less robust building, been totally destroyed. While the damage could have been a great deal worse, and luckily no one had been at home when the fire started, the initial shock of what we found on our return from the ancient Greek and Roman delights of Sicily was hard to assimilate. It can't happen to you. But, like so many other things, it can. And it had.

At first glance the damage did not appear to be so bad. The smell of smoke pervaded the nostrils and made us gag and the acrid fumes stung our eyes, but the apartment itself and its contents – particularly the several thousand books, many of them valuable, seemed to be intact. It was some time later that the reality and extent of what had happened sank in. A finger dragged down what had once been a white wall came away black, the colourful bindings of the books appeared uniformly grey, the sofas and the soft furnishings, the towels and the linens, were impregnated with an odour so pervasive that it would haunt us for many months. A pall of grey smoke obfuscated everything.

Stunned, exhausted from the journey and its unexpected end, and despite explicit warnings from the fire brigade not to do so, we dumped our suitcases and collapsed into bed. How idiotic can you be? The toxic fumes were in the bed and the bedding, the carpets and the curtains. We woke up scarcely able to breathe and had to remove a thick layer of soot from the basin before we could wash – a bath was out of the question – and scour clean, with great difficulty (soot is notoriously hard to remove), every spoon and fork that came out of a blackened drawer before we could attempt to use it. As we stared blankly at a contaminated packet of breakfast cereal and realised that there remained nothing in the cupboard that was fit to eat, the impossibility of our situation began to sink in.

What to do first? We were alive and unharmed but our world had, in the course of a few hours, been turned suddenly upside down. Normal life had been put on hold when we discovered, just in case we did not have enough to cope with, that the firefighters, by accidentally dropping a slab of concrete on it, had crushed my car!

Our insurance company was Chubb, our policy in their 'Masterpiece' range and our payments, fortunately, up to date. In no time at all they sent along their loss assessor, one Mr MacLaren, who at first, while sympathising with our situation, appeared anxious in case we were about to inundate him, and by extension the insurance company, with false and unsupported claims. When in the fullness of time it became apparent that we were not, his demeanour, on his many visits to us, relaxed and he could not have been more helpful in enabling us to sort out the mess in which we found ourselves.

It soon became obvious that we could not stay in the apartment; could not even, in the interests of health and safety, spend another night in it. The only clothes in our possession that were not contaminated by the smoke and would ultimately need either washing, dry-cleaning or in the event that neither was successful, replacing, were in our holiday suitcases. Without bothering to unpack we picked up our highly unsuitable holiday wear, our sun hats and sandals and, having been given permission to do so by Mr MacLaren – who would not only pick up the tab but be in control of our lives and expenditure for the next six months – checked in to the nearby Durrant's Hotel. While not an ideal situation – we had had enough of hotels in the past two weeks and had been looking forward to coming home – we could not have made a better choice.

Unlike your Hiltons and Holiday Inns, whose sterile conformity and ubiquity could be relied upon, Durrant's, unusually, was a privately owned Georgian town-house hotel, which advertised 'comfort, charm and a welcoming experience' to the discerning traveller. Their claims were not unfounded and the hostelry, which had been owned by the Miller family since 1921, sympathised with our plight and, through the efforts of their old-fashioned and traditional staff, made us more than welcome. Stepping, courtesy of Chubb, into the antique-filled suite, complete with a pair of Staffordshire dogs on the mantelpiece and fire irons in the hearth, we had no idea that the short stay for which we had booked would turn out to be six disorientating weeks, after which it would be time, not to return home, but, like the migrants we had become, to move on.

The hotel staff could not have been more accommodating. When they learned that I was a writer they revealed that the hotel had been the haunt of many writers who, having visited the quaint, leather-chaired George Bar, frequently dined there. In 1986 Durrant's had been chosen by the ill-fated Primo Levi as a base for his publicity tour, and in 2007 the American prize-winning author, Howard Norman, had used it as a backdrop for his novel *Devotion*.

While we were not exactly sleeping in cardboard boxes underneath the arches or on the Embankment, it is not until you are rendered homeless (in the broadest sense of the term) that you realise how precious and how generally unappreciated and important to your sanity are a regular place to rest your head and to have your familiar possessions around you. We had few clothes to wear, no favourite books to read, no computers and printers, no personal address books, files and daily paraphernalia that had previously enabled us, unthinkingly, to process our everyday lives. Shaken out of our complacency, we realised how lucky we had been. Not only not to have lost our all in the fire but never, like the growing number of asylum seekers or our own grandparents, to have known displacement or to be in want of a roof over our heads.

As the full extent of the damage to our apartment manifested itself, as did the time and effort it would take to put it to rights, it became obvious that, hospitable as Durrant's Hotel had been, it was impracticable to stay on. The novelty of eating in restaurants or dining with supportive friends and family quickly wore off, and when Mr MacLaren (another

Andrew), recommended that we move to a furnished flat we looked forward both to getting back to our familiar routine and home cooking, and put the wheels in motion to find a suitable one. It was easier said than done.

In no mood to house-hunt, and accompanied by a series of eager and extremely youthful estate agents' runners attached by their umbilical cords to cellphones, we were ferried from one ghastly, sparsely furnished and unkempt letting property – sagging mattresses and nowhere to hang your hat – to another. Our priorities were not so much space for entertaining and fine dining but somewhere to install our computers and a place to park the car. The flat we settled on, out of sheer desperation (in the heady days before the credit crunch the rent was exorbitant but it was not our problem), fulfilled these criteria but, as we were later to discover, nothing worked. Hot water gushed out of the cold tap in the bathroom making teeth cleaning a hazard, neither the telephone line nor the broadband we both required was yet installed, the washing machine was leaking, neither the microwave nor the cooker functioned and the absence of curtains in the bedroom meant that the street lights kept us awake. We had not only to refurbish our old apartment completely but, for the benefit of the landlord – who, luckily for him but tiresomely for us, was holed up in Singapore – to make habitable a property (albeit newly converted and freshly painted) that did not even belong to us.

How accustomed one gets to one's daily and long-standing routine. How abruptly were we shaken out of it. In our own apartment every item of clothing had to be washed or dry-cleaned (anxious to get on with our lives we could not face replacing old and much-loved favourites that had accumulated over years), soft-furnishings had to be renewed (the smell of smoke could not be eradicated), every item of china and glass, carpets and rugs, and a lifetime of possessions restored, a new bed and bedding as well as curtains and carpets estimated for before finally being decided upon and ordered, and the entire apartment had to be redecorated if we were ever to be able to get rid of the smell of smoke, which engulfed you as soon as you opened the front door and even before you did so. The shopping was tiring. Everything you asked for was 'out of stock' and the juvenile salespeople (if you were lucky enough to find one who was not 'at lunch' at ten o'clock in the morning, or 'on their break') had never heard of waste-paper baskets. 'Yer mean, like, for the rubbish? They got bins in Kitchen.'

The days grew into weeks and the weeks into months – factories were closed over Christmas and deliveries delayed – which were spent poring over paint cards and patterns of curtains and carpets and cushions, which we were in no mood to select, and supervising teams of removal men who were taking the books and the furniture and whatever could be salvaged into store, and craftsmen who, although without a word of English, worked their socks off and were not forever listening to a blaring radio while eating their sandwiches or drinking tea.

Preoccupied with the curse of 'possessions', which had accrued over the years, in the midst of which we lived but which had over time become both unimportant and invisible, we were now forced to spend our days, as if setting up home for the first time, in the material world of furnishing and decorating, and neither of us was able to get on with work. There were the inevitable glitches. The various trades got in each other's way and progress was halted; the decorator underestimated the number of rolls of wallpaper required and had to wait for a delivery from Holland, the specialist cleaners left the door of the freezer open over-night causing a minor flood and the kitchen floor (the only one undamaged by the fire) had to be replaced. As we shiv-ered in what had once been our home but had now become a building site, on a daily basis if only to collect the mail, it began to look highly unlikely that we would ever return. We decided that enough was enough and agreed to bite the bullet.

On the day that our new and blissfully comfortable bed was delivered (we had not had the old one very long), we once again packed up the few belongings we had been able to take to the temporary flat and, this time in a 'mini-move', moved back. Despite the daily influx of young Eastern Europeans who smiled charmingly each time you spoke to them although they did not understand a word you said, and the fact that we had to live in the bedroom – the only room marginally habitable – we had finally rid ourselves of our refugee status and what had turned out to be a very much 'furnished to let' property (which we had improved and put into working order for the next tenants) and were once again 'home'.

How had the fire started? Unbelievably, and according to the police who had interrogated everyone living in the block, it had turned out to be arson. The apartment below ours belonged to a mysterious Ukrainian who had neither furnished nor lived in it. The two young student 'house sitters', neither of whom was a suspect, had been at college at the time that an intruder had threatened a cleaner and forced his way in to set fire to their two beds, one at either end of the flat. The terrified cleaner, and only witness, had fled across the park, never to be found, and the arsonist had apparently disappeared. While Scotland Yard patrolled the building on a daily basis for several months, no clues as to the perpetrators of the fire were found and the case was finally closed.

Back in our home again we realised, not for the first time, how lucky we were to live (by accident really, nobody wanted our curious one-bedroomed apartment where the top of the lift cage serves as my desk) in one of the 'lungs of London'. 'Our' park – the residents feel very proprietorial – was not only larger than the Jardin des Plantes and the Luxembourg Gardens put together, but was also the place where, according to French critic and historian Hippolyte Adolphe Taine: '... the vast watery meadows have a charming softness, and the green branches drip with monotonous sound upon the still waters of the pond.' In its time, this royal park has served as a foraging ground for pigs, a mortgage for a king in need, and as farmland supplying the capital. Home to Charles Dickens, it was the birthplace of *David Copperfield*, *Barnaby Rudge* and *A Christmas Carol*, among other immortal works, and in the author's house many of his friends, including William Charles Macready, Thomas Carlyle and William Makepeace Thackeray, were received. Home, too, to Edgar Wallace, H. G. Wells and Elizabeth Bowen – the doyenne of Regent's Park writers – the park was also mentioned lovingly in their works by poets William Wordsworth, W. B. Yeats and Elizabeth Barrett Browning, novelists Henry James and Virginia Woolf and – in our own time – by Alan Bennett, Anita Brookner and P. D. James.

I am afraid of many things – flying, deep waters and loud bangs among others – but fire and immolation have never figured on my list. They still do not. While the whole process, the refurbishing, the tedious meetings with Andrew MacLaren, the shopping and copying and posting of every invoice, receipt and chit was wearying and time-consuming it was not, in the grand order of things, a tragedy. There was little financial loss, no lives sacrificed. At best it was an inconvenience, at worst a shaking up we could well have done without at our time of life. Like assault and burglary it was, as they say, one of the hazards, one of the consequences of twenty-first-century living and of life itself. As far as the downside was concerned, although no one was physically hurt by the fire, it was both stressful and traumatic; the upside was an almost brand-new apartment on which we would have to spend no money for as long as we lived and the experience, fortunately not life-threatening, which is the grist to every writer's mill. Throughout literature – from Homer's *Odyssey* to Miss Havisham's burning wedding dress in *Great Expectations* and the conflagration that engulfed the entire island in *Lord of the Flies* – fire, the bringer of destruction, the symbol of chaos and of war, has been used as metaphor; perhaps, when it has become a distant memory, it will work as such for me.

7

Old Geysers

Travel makes one modest: one sees what a tiny place one occupies in the world.

GUSTAVE FLAUBERT

Like Mrs Disraeli I am hopeless at history and can never remember whether the Greeks came before or after the Romans. I love to travel and my favourite journey is to visit anywhere I haven't been and to return enriched with new experiences, new inspirations and a fresh outlook on what was often, apart from my writing, which takes up most of my time, a pretty mundane life. It was by sheer coincidence that we elected to visit Iceland – the land of cool, soon to turn bitter – only weeks before the volcanic island (now, in the wake of the recently erupting Eyjafjallajköll which temporarily paralysed European airspace, only too familiar) was confronted with bankruptcy and the financial institutions, such as Icesave, Landsbanki and Kaupthing Singer Friedlander (in which we had funds invested), spiralled into meltdown.

Not even the traditional dark cloud, no bigger than a man's hand, was visible on the horizon when, having survived the dark days of my illness, the pleasures of *An Eligible*

Man and the pain of the fire, together with its fallout, we made our plans.

Both of us, fortunately, had always had itchy feet and in our heydays, before mass tourism had made visits to the sights and sounds of the world an endurance test rather than a pleasure, when it had been more a question of stumbling upon remote chapels, little known galleries and unexpected paintings rather than assiduously collecting air-miles, obtaining tickets in advance or queuing for hours to see them (having already had the foresight to book flights a year ahead), we had left our four children with willing relatives, upped sticks, packed our Rohan travelling gear (which dried overnight and was much admired throughout the world, we even had offers for it in China), and taken off for Australia and Alaska, Ireland and India, New York and New Zealand and other parts of the globe.

The sad thing about heydays or periods of greatest vigour is that you neither realise when are you in them nor appreciate them at the time. As travel itself became more complicated, more hedged about with bureaucracy and 'peak seasons' and 'special fares', which one had to press countless buttons, listen to endless music and get up extremely early to secure, we realised that although we had both been too busy chasing our own tails to pay any heed to the passage of time, we were no longer either willing or able to cope with packing and unpacking our suitcases a dozen times in the course of a couple of weeks, to face crack-of-dawn starts or late-night drives on unfamiliar roads, and that, tell it not in Gath, the age of the 'cruise' had arrived.

Young and unafraid, we had always assumed superior smiles when confronted with brochures that depicted tuxe-doed punters drooling over roulette wheels and grey-haired, formally dressed grandparents smiling their dentally enhanced smiles as they waltzed sedately round the floor of some cavernous ship's ballroom. Such alluring images had nothing to do with us. Nor did they. It was by sheer good luck that some years ago we stumbled across MV *Minerva* run by Swan's Discovery Cruises. While in the grand order of things a cruise is still a cruise, *Minerva* promised no louche casino, no gyrating couples, no sycophantic maître d' offering 'fine dining', which looked as if it had been assembled on the plate by some avant-garde artist rather than lovingly cooked. Carrying a maximum of two hundred-odd passengers (rather than the several thousands of traditional cruise ships), the small, yet spacious motor vessel promised imaginative itineraries – to Antarctica and Africa, to the Aegean and the Adriatic, to Greece and Gallipoli – a well-stocked library and a panel of eminent guest speakers each acknowledged in his field and with a talent for bringing his subject, from archaeology to military history and marine biology, to life.

Laugh as you might, as we became less and less mobile *Minerva* suited us. It was the nearest thing to Flaubert's preferred form of travel which was to 'lie on a divan and have the scenery carried past him'.

Why Iceland? Why not? Travel means primarily the discovery of towns and landscapes, and in view of the events of the past months we desperately needed a change of scenery. We had been neither to Iceland, the Orkneys nor the Faroe Islands – all on the ship's itinerary – and August, the month in which we were free to travel, was too hot as far as I was concerned for the more familiar southern hemisphere. While a holiday is (hopefully) a holiday, the run-up to it requires as much planning and strategy as a major battle and, over the years, as I have learned to my cost, you can't plan and execute at the same time.

Determined to use the days 'at sea' to catch up with my reading (to see what my contemporaries were up to) for which there never seemed to be any satisfactory chunks of time at home, where research took precedence over reading for pleasure, my priority was a (virtual) trip to Amazon. co.uk. *Pace* the independent and struggling bookshops – with the owners of which I sympathised but to my shame did not often enough support – how did we ever manage without this colossus, without this behemoth? I found the whole Amazon ritual intensely satisfying and like the best of plays or novels, it had a beginning, a middle and an end. Over the weeks, between these exciting virtual excursions to the warehouse in Milton Keynes, where 10,000 jobs were advertised every month, which was the size of eight football pitches and at the efficient wonders of which I never ceased to marvel, I made a note of any book I wanted to read on my desk diary and marked the page with a red post-it flag. When the time came to put in an order (several books at one time to save on postage) I collected up the titles, added them to my 'shopping basket' and 'hey presto', waited – 'your order should be with you within 3–5 days' – for the postman. The rectangular brown cardboard parcel with its pristine contents arrived on time and the first, most important, and heaviest stage of my Iceland packing was complete.

What did I read? Trying to describe a book you have read is like handing someone a brick to show them what your house looks like. The titles which stood out for me on the Iceland trip were *The Book Thief* by Markus Zusak, an extraordinary story about a nine-year-old girl whose parents have been taken away to a concentration camp in Nazi

Germany and whose compulsion is to steal books; David Lodge's *Deaf Sentence*, which manages to deal poignantly, humorously and entertainingly with the unsung affliction of hearing loss; and Richard Dawkins's *The God Delusion*, which reinforced my view that we can give up belief in God while not losing touch with a treasured heritage.

Packing the books was easy and enjoyable. Packing the clothes and the pills and the potions upon which the quality of life of the average senior citizen is more or less dependent was another matter. Iceland sounded cold but in this age of global warming, which was never out of the newspapers, was it in fact? Did we need shorts and bikinis or sweaters and anoraks? In the event we took both, which was extremely cumbersome, but, since no flights were involved and there were no luggage restrictions, was feasible. Armed with passports, travel insurance and Norwegian and Icelandic krona (NOK and ISK) – today the latter barely worth the paper they are written on – and laden with hedges against every vagary of climate and sufficient sustenance for the mind, we set out for Dover from where *Minerva* was due to sail.

Before they have even started, holidays or short breaks are beneficial. As soon as you shut the front door behind you the worries, most of which you can no longer do anything about, disappear. Already there was a sensation of ataraxia, absence of care. We were on our way.

One of the fallouts from the toxic drugs directed at my cancer was that I was left with 'peripheral neuropathy', an appellation almost as difficult to remember as the 'follicular lymphoma' of the disease itself. This meant that not only were my feet and legs extremely painful (more drugs), but that I had lost some of the sensation in them and when faced with steps or stairs had to rely upon a walking stick. I was not alone. While most of the *Minerva* passengers had little interest in the on-board casinos or midnight buffets of your bog-standard cruise ship, mobility and hearing aids were de rigueur; as experts on Late Norse Culture, calligraphers, civil servants, doctors of divinity and of medicine, Reith Lecturers and Royal Academicians trod their careful way up the gangplank and were welcomed on board by the captain, into whose hands we were to put our lives for the next two weeks, the security cameras captured their mugshots.

The ports of call were unfamiliar and in some cases unpronounceable: Flåm (in Norway), Tórshaven (the Faroe Islands), Seyðisfjörður and Heimaey (Iceland). Having gone from our well-appointed cabin (everything shipshape and complete with orchids) to our designated muster station in the Darwin Lounge for the compulsory lifeboat drill with which we were familiar from our past *Minerva* trips to Vietnam and Cambodia and to the Black Sea, we were free to enjoy our fifteen days in limbo where there were no grid-locked roads, no carbon emissions, no mail or telephones demanding to be answered (although a business centre was available), no meals to be planned and cooked, no deadlines clamouring to be met.

Our cabin stewardess, Galina, made us welcome. A fifteen-stone, six-foot-tall Russian, menacing as the babushkas who had once policed the corridors of Moscow hotels, she shook our hands and in the few words of English at her disposal assured us that she had put some 'vater' in our cabin and that if we 'vanted anysing' she was at our disposal. While the crew of the *Minerva* were mainly European – the Captain was Italian – the 'hotel' staff were from every part of the globe and delightful they were too. Despite the fact that gratuities, which were included in the price of the trip, were strictly forbidden, nothing was too much trouble. In a few hours (although the ship had only just returned from the last cruise) they knew every passenger, together with their special needs, by name and were always ready with a helping hand for the oldies when the MV *Minerva*, despite its excellent stabilisers, was on a roll.

The lectures, three a day, were given in the Darwin Lounge but could be seen, too, in the cinema – where church services and Roman Catholic Mass were also held – or on the cabin TV: the quality of the talks with their slide shows and PowerPoint presentations was such that they were as packed to capacity at the end of the voyage as they had been at the beginning.

The first port of call was the small town of Flåm, surrounded by steep mountainsides, roaring waterfalls and deep valleys, the approach to which was through Sognefjord, a dramatic glacial gash through Norway's Caledonian mountains. While those passengers who elected to stay on board were offered screenings of recent films in the cinema or in the cabins, or could spend the day at leisure, we made our way by ship's tender (not as easy at it sounds) to the beautiful small town as far removed from the urban congestion to which we were accustomed as it was possible to be.

The Flåmsbana (Flåm Railway) which took twenty years to complete, which crosses the narrow Flåm valley and which is definitely not your Bakerloo or Piccadilly Line, is one of the steepest railway lines in the world. With its gradient of 1:18 on almost eighty per cent of the line it is regarded as a masterpiece of Norwegian engineering. From Myrdal, on the Hardangervidda plateau, to Flåm in the innermost corner of the Aurlandfjord, the train travels almost vertically through some of Norway's most breathtaking scenery: rivers that bisect deep ravines, waterfalls that cascade down the sides of steep, snow-capped mountains and farms seeming to cling precariously to sheer slopes.

Sensibly, and catering for every age and every degree of physical fitness and mobility, the shore excursions at the various ports of call (included in the price of the cruise fare) were graded. Gone were the days when we could hike or trek for more than two hours over rough, uneven or slippery ground with no handrails on the steps and no toilets. If Grade 5 was a no-no, Grade 4, with its full-day tours and substantial levels of activity was not much better. Grade 3 with its lengthy site visits and no opportunity to return to the coach, was borderline, and in the end, to be on the safe side and so that we did not disgrace ourselves, we opted for Grade 2 with its absence of steep gradients and ten-minute walks over easy terrain.

The weather, miraculously, was on our side. While the UK shivered and sheltered beneath umbrellas, the temperature was unusually 39°C (shorts) in the clutch of islands that was the Hanseatic city of Bergen with its picturesque wooden wharf buildings, its backdrop of seven mountains and its two celebrated Edvards, Munch and Grieg. Of course, as the purists insist, a whistle-stop tour by cruise passengers, by its very nature is no way to see the world. What about King Olav Kyrre who in 1070 gave Bergen, already a major port, its royal charter? What about the Middle Ages when the Black Death which swept over Europe devastated Norway as half the population succumbed to the pestilence? Many weeks, months, years could be spent in each place we visited, cherry-picking from the plethora of sights and sounds and museums and galleries, from Norway's rich and varied history.

Of course we had our lectures, which prepared us in no little measure for the surface of places which – sometimes in a day, sometimes in a few days – we were barely able to scratch. It was better than nothing. Better than staying at home. It whetted our appetites. We could always, in an ideal world, come back.

Streymoy, Eysturoy, Vágoy, Sandøy, Borðoy and Svínoy: the Faroes, an eerily treeless archipelago of eighteen volcanic islands in the heart of the Gulf Stream, which were stalked by pilot whales and were home to guillemots, kittiwakes, puffins and Arctic tern, were familiar only from the radio: 'Faroes, Fair Isle, Fastnet and Forties ...' We would never listen to the shipping forecasts again without feeling the westerly winds so strong that toads, reptiles and land mammals gave the islands a wide berth, and the only rodents to be found arrived by chance and by ship.

While Bergen, Flåm and the unforgettable windswept beauty of the Faroes whose sparse, churchgoing population (47,511), mainly of fisherman, lived equably with the daily fear of earthquakes and eruptions of basalt larva (they simply got out and moved house) whet our appetites, Iceland, of which we had heard so much and in today's financial crisis have heard even more, was the icing on the *Minerva* cake.

Fortunately for us, on few tourist trails, Iceland is renowned for its startling landscapes (soul food), its hot springs and its geysers. It lies on the Mid-Atlantic Ridge – a divergent tectonic plate boundary located along the floor of the Atlantic Ocean – which separates the Eurasian Plate and North American Plate and is slowly but surely, at a rate of ten centimetres a year, widening the gulf between North America and Europe.

Never did I think that I would be interested in geology, but this brief glimpse of a part of the world I had never visited not only increased my respect for Charles Darwin but took me back, like a time traveller, 400 million years – the sea lamprey pre-dated the dinosaur by a mere 250 million years – to some of the most important events in the history of our planet as our lives, 'solitary, poor, nasty, brutish and short' according to philosopher Thomas Hobbes, leaped into awe-inspiring perspective.

Iceland, situated as it is right on the Rift, is unique; everywhere else along the Rift volcanic activity takes place on the seabed, but for seventeen million years white steam has hissed and spumed its way through the thin crust of the earth and Iceland's volcanoes have risen above the waters, causing eruptions powerful enough to propel ash as far as the stratosphere – as we know to our cost today – and hot springs, including the renowned 'Geysir' (from which we get our 'geyser') arise from fissures small enough to jump over and large enough to form wide valleys (Thingvillir National Park).

Seyðisfjörður, Heimaey and Reykjavik, names and places to conjure with. Gullfoss – one of the most dramatic waterfalls in Europe – and the geothermically heated waters of the blue lagoon; the family sagas of Icelandic literature with their mythical trolls and elves whose mischievous exploits are given credence by eighty per cent of the islanders; delicacies such as the meat of a basking shark, cured and hung to dry for four to five months, boiled sheep's head, and ram's testicles pickled in whey to be found in every home. The population of Iceland, with its lucrative cod-trawling grounds, have a life expectancy of 81.3 years for women and 76.4 years for men and had one of the highest standards of living in the world until the banking crisis and the eruption in the global financial market left them with crippling debts and there was a very real danger that the economy could be sucked into the whirlpool. With a passion for music, many communities have their own choirs. Gunnar Gunnarsson of Valthjófsstaður (although writing in Danish) was their literary hero with his poetry, fiction and plays while Iceland's own Halldór Laxness, now largely forgotten, won the Nobel Prize for literature in 1955.

St Magnus Cathedral on the Orkney Island of Kirkwall, giant rhododendrons from China, gum trees from Australia and climbers from Chile in the micro-climate of Inverewe Garden – where gardeners were shrouded in green mosquito nets to protect them from the marauding midges – in the breathtaking Scottish Highlands rounded off our trip.

Disembarking at Dover, where already vast containers of fresh fruit and vegetables were being winched aboard for the next voyage, we returned to reality. While to the *echt* traveller the fifteen-day *Minerva* cruise might have seemed like a cop-out, for a couple of octogenarians it ticked every box. The informal restaurant (as distinct from the Dining Room with its special sense of occasion), the Veranda, meant that passengers were free to choose from the widest possible variety of well-cooked food of every nationality, the seating was open, inside or outside on deck (weather permitting) and at breakfast, lunch, dinner and tea, lasting friendships (for the sociable) were made over bacon and eggs or scones and jam. The well-stocked library, an oasis of peace for the serious readers always to be found with their noses in *Exploring the World of the Vikings, Volcanoes and Society, Whales and Dolphins* or other books relating to destinations visited, was both appreciated and well-used, while the state-of-the-art gymnasium and the Promenade Deck (eight circuits to a mile) catered to the more athletically minded of the passengers. The birdwatchers (binoculars thoughtfully provided in every cabin) watched birds, while the whale watchers watched whales. The swimmers (bravely for the most part) swam in the minuscule pool, the photographers took photographs and the guest speakers fraternised and took questions from the curious and entered into illuminating discussions with the informed. In wellworn windcheaters beneath sun hats which had seen both many parts of the world and better days, we found artists and writers, men of law and of letters, geologists, physicists, captains of industry and parliamentarians. Mobility and hearing aids were forgotten as other worlds were explored and new friendships forged. While the majority of the passengers were long retired from their life's work, they had not left their brains or their sense of wonderment behind them. For them, as for us, as we bade farewell to our captain and made our final and slow way down the gangplank, *Fjords, Faroes & Iceland* had not only done the job of restoring our equilibrium after the traumas of the past few months but had been an outstanding success.

8

Things ...

Unless you catch ideas on the wing and nail them down, you will soon cease to have any.

VIRGINIA WOOLF

'... Note it in a book, that it may be for the time to come for ever and ever.' In accordance with this admonition from Isaiah and in common with many other writers, when I come across a phrase, sentence or passage in a book that strikes a chord in me and which I want to remember I write it down. The repositories for these *bons mots* which I come across during the course of my reading is a collection of hard-backed notebooks in varying colours, feint-ruled and measuring twelve by eight inches. Little did I think when I started this compulsive anthology many years ago that the 3,000-plus entries in seven volumes would ever see the light of day or that they would be anything other than for my eyes only.

According to Pablo Picasso, if one knew exactly what one was going to do there would be not much point in doing it. I had no idea that the steadily growing collection of random quotations would be of interest to anyone other than myself, only that the cardinal rule behind such a compilation was that the moment one comes across an opinion/sentence/ passage/aphorism one wishes to retain it must be torn out/ copied/memorised/noted immediately. If time is allowed to elapse through laziness, indolence or lack of a handy pen or pencil, the precise publication cannot be recalled, the page number is forgotten and no matter how hard one searches for them the wise words are lost for ever. That the entries were handwritten in notebooks, rather than efficiently recorded in some appositely named computer file, is testimony to the visceral fact that the idiosyncratic look of handwritten words, the satisfaction of making marks on paper has, for one writer at least, despite the cataclysmic and inevitable progress of technology, not lost its appeal. The fact that the sayings, entered sometimes in haste, cannot always be easily deciphered is neither here nor there. There is still pleasure to be gained from forming a letter rather than hitting a key, from causing ink to flow, words to arrange themselves into sentences followed by the name of the author, the title of the work where the entry may be found, and – most importantly – by the page number in the particular edition on your bookshelf. It is for this reason that whenever possible I like to buy my books – the endpapers of which are filled with pencilled columns of page numbers afterwards transferred to my notebooks – rather than borrow them from the library where to mark the text is not only antisocial but is strictly *verboten*.

For want of a better title my collection was called *Things ...* I considered the project sufficiently unimportant not to mention it and told no one about the words of wisdom I was amassing concurrently with whatever I happened to be writing. *Things ...* was a distillation of received ideas from deceased or contemporary writers on such diverse topics as life and death, books and literature, reading and religion, creativity and travel: insights expressed in such a way that one wished one had written them oneself. Often we do not know what we think until we see it written down and these collected thoughts of the wise and witty have fuelled my novels, facilitated my research, filled my idle moments, confirmed my prejudices and enriched my life.

'All those who live as literary men – working as literary labourers – will agree with me that three hours a day will produce as much as a man ought to write.' If Anthony Trollope hadn't given me permission to leave my desk after three hours' concentrated work I would have felt guilty about doing so. He is absolutely correct in his assumption that anything above a three-hour stint, for me at any rate, is counterproductive. But how eloquently put. How wise.

'You once said that you would like to sit beside me while I write. Listen, in that case I could not write at all … one can never be alone enough when one writes, why there can never be enough silence around one when one is writing, why even night is not night enough.' Not night enough! How movingly Franz Kafka explains the sensitivity of the writer's soul to distraction of the slightest sort. In order for the floodgates to open one has to take the first tentative steps into another world, one in which the words, by some unseen and magical process, flow from brain to hand to screen or paper with no thought or explanation of exactly how it is done. The sound of other human beings within earshot, the demands or even the sight of loved ones, can be enough to interrupt the flow, to cause the well to dry as one returns to quite another plane, concerns oneself with the mundane preoccupations of the everyday. That 'writers are a scourge to those they cohabit with …' was plain to Irish writer, Edna O'Brien. 'They are present and at the same time they are absent. They are present by the fact of their continuing curiosity, their observing, their cataloguing minds, their longing to see into another person. But the longing is discharged into the work.' It's true. We are hard to live with: there but not there. Always there are two of us: the one who functions in the real world, going about one's business, answering queries and telephones, resolving problems, taking necessary steps, yet all the while squirrelling away sights and sounds and human beings, known and unknown, later to be cannibalised, inwardly digested with no particle wasted and transformed into prose. We live a two-tiered existence, inhabit other planets. Little wonder we are always tired.

The authors acknowledged in my books of commonplaces – for that is what they are – reflect the random nature of my reading. Maimonides, Marcel Proust and Oscar Wilde rub shoulders with Graham Greene, Simone de Beauvoir, Sam Goldwyn, Doris Lessing and Gabriel García Márquez. There are sound bites from playwrights: '... a script usually gets worse from the first draft on ...' from the successful David Mamet, from whom I also learned that 'Good drama has no stage directions'; prejudice from Friedrich Nietzsche: 'The crowd has taken possession of places, which were created by civilization for the minority, for the best people'; encouragement from Emerson: 'He has not learnt the lesson of life who does not every day surmount a fear'; while according to Mario Vargos Llosa, 'Commonplaces are put to use only by imbeciles or geniuses ...' and 'Mediocre natures avoid them ...'

The commonplace book emerged in the early Renaissance period and usually took the form of a writer's notebook in which were recorded apposite quotations from other writers that were by turns inspirational, motivational, philosophical or meditative. This resulted in a book that was not merely a miscellany, but a unique reflection of the compiler's thoughts and mind. By keeping an account of the key points of his readings, he made a journal of his own, stamped with his personality. Not until I had amassed some three thousand-odd quotations did I realise that the collection as a whole was an exact reflection of my thoughts and feelings. I made up my mind to do something about it.

What I decided was to have the quotations typed up and in this more legible form to leave them as a legacy of what was on my mind, to give some idea of what had made their mother tick to my four daughters.

The typist, Susan Close, was painstaking. Not many people would have undertaken the mammoth task, deciphering my shorthand in places, working out the precise location of the 'ibids' where the quotations were to be found, culling frequent repetitions and sorting out a numerical order that often went haywire. It was a long (and costly) job, and something she kindly undertook to do in the pockets of free time available between her regular (and more straightforward) commissions.

When the work was completed, during which time I was finding a publisher for my novel, *Paris Summer*, and looking forward to a production of my 'transplant' play *Change of Heart* in Houston, Texas, the commonplace book looked interesting enough to have another life and I set about exploiting its unexpected potential – in the vernacular to try to get it published.

Like most, if not all, writers, I was no stranger to rejection and had learned long ago that the name of the game is endurance. The buzzword in novels at this particular time was Lionel Shriver's (a woman with a man's name) *We Need to Talk About Kevin,* a brilliant epistolary novel written by a mother trying to make sense of why her son shoots seven students in the school gym and watches with grim satisfaction as his classmates bleed to death. *We Need to Talk About Kevin* was rejected by the author's own agent and thirty publishers before Serpent's Tail picked it up and made Lionel Shriver a literary superstar. I was not after stardom, merely publication for the collection of wise words I guessed would interest many readers. While it was true that the genre was no longer popular, I was not deterred. The only commonplace book that sprang to mind was John Julius Norwich's *Christmas Crackers,* a personal collection of quirky quotes and literary odds and ends, which he sends to his friends instead of Christmas cards. Every decade Penguin brings out an unillustrated collection of these and now Quentin Blake (who illustrated my two children's books) had made his own selection from his favourite pieces, illustrated them in his inimitable style and published them with Doubleday.

The only other similar book I was aware of was *A Gentleman Publisher's Commonplace Book*, compiled by the publisher John G. Murray (John Murray VI) commonly known as Jock. The book, legendary in his lifetime, was first published (by John Murray Publishers Ltd, of course) in 1996 and is still in print. While John Murray, however, accepted the favourite quotations of his authors and many famous friends, including Arthur Rackham and John Piper, my prized collection was my own. Unfortunately I did not have my own publishing house at my disposal – how useful it would have been if I had – and had to push for *Things ...* both by myself and through my agent Heather Chalcroft.

Things …, not altogether surprisingly, was initially rejected by seven publishers, three of them 'sight unseen', which meant that they were not sufficiently interested in the project to read the manuscript and dumped it straight back on my (or rather Heather's) doorstep. My friend and erstwhile publisher (*A Second Wife*, *To Live in Peace* and *An Eligible Man*) Judy Piatkus, founder and managing director of Piatkus Books, was warm and sympathetic. 'There are wonderful sayings here and you clearly have a marvellous resource … I would happily spend all day browsing in it …' Despite this she wasn't keen to put her money where her mouth was.

It was Toby Buchan, editorial director of Michael O'Mara Books (publisher of the best-selling *Diana Her True Story* by Andrew Morton) and kinsman of the renowned John Buchan (*The Thirty-Nine Steps*), who finally, and to my great surprise, made a 'small offer', small not least because it was a 'risky project' and there was a surfeit of miscellany or companion-style titles on the market at the moment. 'Despite this relatively modest offer …' which was not all that modest as far as I was concerned, he went on to say, 'I do think the book is well done, and its author is undoubtedly an interesting and astute writer, widely read and with a very keen eye as well as a sense of irony.'

The irony was that in the event Michael O'Mara Books Ltd shot themselves in the foot by insisting – it's what publishers do – that I change the title! I have a running joke with author David Lodge. Unbeknownst to each other we both, concurrently, wrote *The Writing Game*, mine a work of non-fiction and his a play, followed by *Home Truths* both of which were plays. Now David had published *Thinks...*, which was as near as you could get to *Things...* The *zeitgeist* was working overtime. Not for Toby Buchan, who wanted to change my title to *A Writer's Commonplace Book*, which was 'easier to categorize for the bookseller'. How wrong he was. When the result of my many years' work finally saw the light of day in what was a most beautifully produced little volume with wonderful and thoughtfully chosen illustrations, the booksellers – other than Foyle's who put it on their Xmas table and the prestigious Heywood Hill – secreted it away in the 'how-to' section for *writers* rather than placing it by the tills for the edification of the general public.

The title was misleading. Although *A Writer's Commonplace Book* was 'by' a writer it was not 'for' writers as the unfortunate title implied. I should have stood my ground but in view of the rejections I had received I was in no position to do so. Despite excellent reviews – 'The book makes compulsive reading ... the literary equivalent of a really expensive box of Belgian chocolates ...' (*Daily Express*); 'A reflective and cerebral anthology' (*Spectator*); 'It is the perfect bedside book ...' (David Lodge); 'Without fail I gain comfort or inspiration from *A Writer's Commonplace Book*' (Shirley Conran) – the book did not sell in the numbers in which it should have done. While I was happy to have my miscellany published at all, much of the print run had to be remaindered and although greatly appreciated by buyers who managed to make their way to the upper floors of the bookshops where it was hidden away, usually in an insignificant bookcase, it was hardly a commercial success.

There was one more bone of contention over which I had to give way. According to Jock Murray: 'The true nature of a commonplace book is the random nature of its contents.' At the insistence of Michael O'Mara I was forced to put my quotations, which I still continue to collect, into pigeonholes:

'On Writers and Writing'; 'On Literary Endeavour'; 'On the Human Condition'; 'On Love, Marriage and Family'; 'On Life and Death' etc. Perhaps Toby Buchan was right here, although compartmentalising the aphorisms quite destroyed the nature of the book. Who knows? I should be grateful I suppose that the contents of my seven hardback notebooks finally – and unexpectedly after so many years' work – made it into print, that I had a substantial sum of money to show for it, and several hundred remaindered copies – useful for birthday and Christmas presents – in my attic. Having decided to publish, the results were not quite what I had anticipated. But then what is?

9

The Bottom Line

*The name of the game is endurance. I've seen a lot of writers
drop away after a few decent stories and disappear.*

TED SOLOTAROFF

Whatever anyone may tell you to the contrary, the majority
of books (except those by best-selling genre authors whose
next reliable and predictable work is eagerly awaited by an
expectant public), plays, and films in particular, languish
for months and often for a great many years before they see
the light of day. With money, rather than literary excellence,
as the bottom line for publishers, artistic directors and film
producers, it is by no means always to do with the quality
of the work. It's not a bit of use trying to climb aboard a
bandwagon that has long passed. Success, or the lack of it, is
often dictated by the ever-changing demands of fashion, the
high turnover of editors (who 'love your work') in publishing houses, and the ephemeral needs of the film industry
whose target audience is usually an extremely fickle 12A.

In common with most other writers – I think I could
safely say *all* – I could paper the walls with rejection slips
that vary from the rave – 'all of us loved it but it doesn't fit
in with our plans at the moment' – to the downright rude

as you get up the nose of an editor fresh from the English department of some erstwhile polytechnic, young enough to be your granddaughter and unable to spell.

Even Charlotte Brontë had to learn the publishing game. Her first novel *The Professor* was turned down by several editors and was published only posthumously, while *Jane Eyre* was rejected on five occasions before it was published under a pseudonym to decidedly lukewarm reviews. A hundred years ago Kenneth Grahame's *The Wind in the Willows* was dismissed in the *Times Literary Supplement* as 'a book with scarcely a smile in it', which 'Grown up readers will find … monotonous and elusive; children will hope in vain for more fun', and in 1859 Edward Fitzgerald, renowned for his English verse translation of *Rubáiyát of Omar Khayyám, the Astronomer Poet of Persia* (which on publication received one review), had himself to pay for a print run of 250 copies of which he retained forty. Bernard Quaritch, antiquarian and oriental bookseller, later agreed to put his own imprint on 210 copies and distribute it for the price of one shilling out of which Fitzgerald did not receive one penny. Although Fitzgerald did give away a few copies to friends and to literary figures of his acquaintance – including Thomas Carlyle, Alfred Lord Tennyson and William Makepeace Thackeray – in the hope of attracting some attention, he seemed modestly reconciled to what was to become one of the best-known poems in the English language being stillborn. It was not until after his death, however, in 1883, that his translation of the *Rubáiyát* became the rage and today, never out of print, a first edition is safely expected to fetch something in the region of £27,000.

As far as rejections are concerned, optimists tend to bounce back more quickly than pessimists. Fortunately I am an optimist. I believe that good will come out of everything and that all you have to do to succeed is to keep on trying. Writers and those in the media know that rejection is implicit in the terms and conditions, and will have developed practical strategies to cope with it. A steely foundation of self-belief is what keeps many writers going. Determination is as important as talent and you learn early on to keep faith with yourself. If you take rejection too much to heart and brood upon it, it will eat away at the creative process.

Despite its topical subject matter summed up by a character in the play: 'I know organs are available. I am not going to wait quietly in line while someone round here plays God!', despite favourable comments from actresses Juliet Stevenson ('a wonderful script') and Anna Massey ('Most powerful script I've ever read. Incredibly commercial. Tender, domestic, painful, philosophical … A goldmine'), *Change of Heart*, my second play, did not find a theatre willing to take it on. Having spent months haunting the relevant departments of the hospitals and researching the subject matter, and considering myself almost ready to qualify as a heart-lung transplant surgeon, I was unwilling to let my hard-earned knowledge go to waste. Refusing to be beaten, I transformed the material into a novel with the title *Intensive Care*.

Having finished the novel, which I thoroughly enjoyed writing (largely, I suspect because I had already researched the material and had everything at my fingertips) a publisher had to be found. This was in the hands of my then agent, Sonia Land of Sheil Land Ltd. Before we knew it we not only had a publisher but a real 'turn-up for the book'. The newly founded House of Stratus '… hugely enjoyed your novel' and 'thought it one of the most sensitive and intelligent fictional treatments of serious illness that I have ever read'. They not only offered a substantial advance for *Intensive Care* but wanted to buy my entire backlist of eighteen novels (many of the early ones out of print) for a very large sum of money indeed. It was akin to having several birthdays rolled into one and I applauded Sonia for her coup. When an article appeared in the *Sunday Times* with the news that Joan Collins was to receive a six-figure advance after signing up with David Lane, the owner of the recently floated House of Stratus Ltd, I thought I was on to a good thing. Little did I know!

David Lane was not only the man responsible for bringing the popular children's character, little Noddy, back to life but launched the first publishing house to use the latest high technology in printing. House of Stratus, with its IBM machines, would be the first in the field to print 'books on demand', ensuring that warehouses piled high with books, and the dreaded words 'out of print' would become a thing of the past. In a first for a UK publishing company, House of Stratus would enter the United States market from day one. This then unique strategy was destined to ensure that all titles, new or reissued, were marketed on a continual basis. The company had signed up the backlists of a wide range of well-known authors – including Nevil Shute, Joyce Cary, Nicholas Monsarrat, C. P. Snow and Dan Jacobson – as well as agents and authors from around the world prepared to license valuable and well-known intellectual property rights. According to their newsletter, House of Stratus had a tie-in with Steven Spielberg for his new film *Artificial Intelligence* (AI) and had signed a contract with Auberon Waugh to reissue his autobiography and five of his novels. My own titles featured prominently in the newsletter. Lane, who was previously managing director of Enid Blyton (the subsidiary of Chorian that owned the rights to Enid Blyton's books), aimed to establish House of Stratus as a major player in publishing for the new millennium.

So far, so good. Several of my early novels were already out of print and had been for some time, and I was hard put to produce copies for the House of Stratus's new edition. Friends and family were unwilling to relinquish their signed copies, even though I promised they would be returned, and I had to have a quick whip round the websites of a few second-hand booksellers. Having, amazingly, managed to track down all the backlist titles, I sent them, together with the completed manuscript of my new novel *Intensive Care* (front list) to this maverick and innovative new publisher from whom I promptly received, via Sonia Land, the agreed monies, publication dates and the usual editorial queries such as: 'Are obliterative bronchitis and obliterative bronchiolitis the same or interchangeable, and why had I given the transplant surgeon's Italian wife a Spanish name?' The jacket roughs were delivered promptly and on time, and were delightful, I put the wheels in motion for my habitual publishing party and everything, so far, was going according to plan. I was on the crest of a wave.

Pushing the boat out, as far as the usually cautious publishing fraternity was concerned, David Lane had lashed out on a mansion in Mayfair as the flagship headquarters for his newly launched company. Accustomed to the statutory glass of inferior wine and sausage-on-a-stick in the dingy boardrooms of the majority of publishers, I was amazed at the splendour of the House of Stratus premises, just refurbished in glass and chrome, and the lavishness of the cocktail party to which all new (living) House of Stratus authors were invited. Jostled by the great and the good, who thronged the many rooms and the elegant staircase, and thinking that this was the new face of publishing, I tucked into the state-of-the-art canapés – made by one of London's major (and most expensive) caterers – which appeared, artfully arranged on silver salvers, with astonishing frequency. It was a very long way from the days of the 'sausage-on-a-stick'.

True to their word, House of Stratus brought out my backlist in a uniform edition with each jacket in a different colour and tastefully illustrated. *Intensive Care* was also produced on the agreed date and David Lane, together with many of his editors and PR staff, came to the publication party which, by tradition, I always gave at home. The most important guest at the party was Julia Polak together with her husband Professor Daniel Catovski, an oncologist-haematologist at the Brompton Hospital. Professor Magdi Yacoub, the surgeon who had carried out Julia's heart-lung transplant and had given his blessing to *Intensive Care*, was invited but was unable to attend.

At about this time the Tissue Engineering Centre at the Chelsea and Westminster Hospital was setting up a new charity, the Julia Polak Research Trust, in the charge of the late Lady Rhys Williams. The Trust was established to help fund research into ways of addressing the terrible realities of transplant surgery, to help those who had received heart-lung transplants and to stimulate the desperately short supply of donor organs, which was responsible for the deaths of one in ten people waiting for a heart, lung, or heart-lung transplant, and the one thousand patients a year who died whilst playing the life-or-death waiting game. As a new 'expert' on the subject I was invited to join the committee of the JPRT. While House of Stratus declared themselves unable to link a donation to the Trust from the sales of the book, I undertook to give a proportion of my royalties to the very worthy cause and Julia, now the longest surviving heart-lung transplantee, became the book's ambassador. No one who was ushered into the professor's room at the Chelsea and Westminster was allowed to leave without buying a copy of *Intensive Care*. Such were her charisma and powers of persuasion that few visitors, medical or otherwise, dared to argue. A large number of copies were offloaded in this way and the funds of the Trust swelled. Fund-raising soirées, both in London and the country, were also held, together with concerts, recitals and other money-making events.

There is a pecking order among literary reviewers. The field was led by books from established publishing giants such as Faber, Cape, Random House and Transworld, and the unknown newcomer to the field, House of Stratus, was not only at the bottom of the pile but had brought out *Intensive Care* in 'trade paperback' (midway between hardback and paperback), a format upon which, at the time, literary editors looked down their noses. Knowing the name of the game, I was philosophical about the lack of newspaper and magazine coverage. While no writer can afford to dismiss the power of the favourable review, and a wall of my study is filled with scrapbooks of newspaper reviews of my previous books, I was not dismayed. It is the reactions of readers who are moved to write to you which gladden an author's heart and the book was not only extremely well and enthusiastically received but encouraged readers to get donor cards.

Everything was going swimmingly until some months later an article in the *Bookseller* was brought to my attention and a chill wind began to blow:

House of Stratus seeks cash: House of Stratus was in talks with potential investors this week to secure further funding after delays with prepress and production left it out of pocket. David Lane, chief executive, said: 'It was probably me getting my sums wrong about how long it would take and how much money was needed to get 2,000 books into print. It's not a big deal.'

It was the understatement of the year and was followed, as the months passed, by:

House of Stratus beset by delays ... The company, which specialises in printing out-of-print titles on demand, reported operating and pre-tax losses of about £1.6m for the year ... half the company's staff has left in the last six months ...

It was clear to my agent, Sonia Land, who had in good faith got me into this, although at the time not to me, that there was 'something rotten in the state of Denmark'.

When House of Stratus was delisted from the London Stock Exchange, the Mayfair headquarters were closed and the firm went into administrative receivership it became obvious that as far as my backlist and *Intensive Care* were concerned, all was far from well. Although, in some Machiavellian plot, the now elusive David Lane had bought the assets of Stratus Holdings Ltd from the administrators and kept open its Yorkshire printworks, there were very few chestnuts to be pulled from that particular ill-conceived fire. Fellow authors who had signed contracts for their new books (destined never to see the light of day) with House of Stratus complained bitterly at David Lane's treatment of them, and agents such as my own refused to have anything more to do with them. True to form, even as his ship was sinking, David Lane angered his many creditors – who had been left high and dry – by having a flamboyantly decorated stand at the London Book Fair, from which he offered extravagant glasses of champagne to passing punters.

An article which appeared in *Private Eye*, under the heading 'Market Farces', delivered the *coup de grâce*:

Last summer, the original company Stratus Holdings PLC went into receivership, owing millions of pounds to authors, agents and print machinery suppliers. Last October the assets were bought from the receivers at a knockdown price by House of Stratus Ltd – a company run by David Lane, the man who had founded the original Stratus and run it into the ground. The deal meant that Lane could carry on trading, unencumbered by his massive debts, and that the poor sods who were owed by the old company had to carry on dealing with him if they were to have any hope of seeing any cash. That slender hope has receded. The new company has gained a reputation as the worst payer in publishing; and the same authors, agents and manufacturers are owed even more … Will it be long before the receivers are called in again?

To be fair, Sonia Land, who some time earlier had seen the writing on the wall, advised me to pull out while the going was good and to have nothing more to do either with David Lane or his new company with whom she refused to contemplate further dealings. Not, at the time, being in possession of all the facts, and anxious, like any author, to get my new novel, *Tsunami* – which David Lane had agreed to publish, although as yet I had no contract – into print as soon as possible, I did not take her advice.

Writers do not write about what has happened but what is going to happen. In 2003 few people had heard the term 'tsunami' and even fewer knew what it actually meant. In chapter one of my new novel, I had to explain the fact that 'tsunami' (a metaphor as far as my story was concerned) was a Japanese word meaning 'harbour wave' or – inaccurately for tides play no part – 'tidal wave', and that when an earthquake occurred offshore it could bring about a sudden change in the shape of the ocean floor. This change caused a massive displacement of water, which in turn produced a powerful wave – or series of waves – that spreads out in all directions. Today, of course, unfortunately, following the horrendous disaster in the Indian Ocean, tsunami has entered the vernacular and even if I had the insensitivity to use the word, no explanation would be needed.

Having had a firm commitment from House of Stratus to publish *Tsunami,* although no contract had as yet been signed, and with all my backlist, as I thought, in print for posterity, I confidently set about starting my next project. It was a surprise to me, although of course not to Sonia Land, when I received a curt fax from David Lane to the effect that in the present financial climate he was no longer willing to stock my backlist and would not now be publishing *Tsunami.* This blow, for which despite Sonia's warnings I had been unprepared, was only marginally mitigated by the fact that my eighteen reissued titles, together with their jacket images, were now on disc in Quark form (print ready) and would be sent to me in due course.

Left high and dry, as far as publishers were concerned, and with a new novel on my hands, I picked myself up and dusted myself down for what was not the first time.

10

Idiot Box

Television is a fantasy which destroys everything.

MALCOLM MUGGERIDGE

I had written before for TV: the pilot for *Shrinks*, a misbe-gotten series of which only the first episode got made, and the commissioned six one-hour episodes of *An Eligible Man*, which also bit the dust but provided the basis for my later eponymous play. I had never seen, and indeed had never heard of, *Doctors*, which aired on BBC at two p.m. every day, with a loyal audience and substantial ratings. On the basis of having written *Intensive Care*, a 'medical' play – the (as yet unperformed) *Change of Heart* – as well as five novels about the early days of the National Health Service, being the wife of a doctor and having spent the first fifteen years of married life as dogsbody in the surgery attached to our first house, I was invited, via my agent, and innocent of the countless hoops, storylines and treatments I would have to go through, to try my hand at writing an episode for the long-running programme. The series revolved around a busy general practice. It consisted of self-contained, character-driven stories, with one of the GPs at the heart of the story driving the action. It was not so much a question of the 'disease of the day', as a story of how the characters' lives are affected by the medical aspect of what they are going through. A minimum of six outline ideas had to be submitted well in advance of the next date on which the series producer would be reading them. Should one of the ideas be accepted, the writer would then be required to write a 'scene-by-scene' synopsis to include the serial element of the programme, which would be given to her at the time. Only if the 'scene by scene' was accepted by the producer would the episode be commissioned.

There was no limit to the number of ideas one could submit. Although the brief sounded intriguing and a piece of cake to an established writer well versed in medical matters, I had no idea of what I was letting myself in for or that not only the story editor but the producer, the director, a couple of executive producers and even a couple of actors would have input into the script. By the time I had finished with *Doctors* the people at the top, flushed with power rather than creativity, would not only have had my guts for garters but fail to acknowledge the very many hours of work I had put in beyond the call of duty. Blithely unaware that writers of the series were expected, as a matter of course, to do many drafts, each of which would go through the same long-winded process, I watched a few tapes of previous episodes sent to me by the assistant script editor, submitted six outline ideas of my own for Series 5, Episode 89, from my stash of medical knowledge – much of it first hand – and waited. And waited. After several months during which I had quite forgotten about the programme and assumed that my suggestions were not 'what they were looking for', one of my ideas, which had to do with the extremely sad 'battered baby' syndrome that caused so much family heartache, was,

to my utter amazement, accepted. Based upon this accept-
ance, but before any contract was signed, I started on the
scene-by-scene breakdown that was required before any
money changed hands.

This was not as easy as it sounded and took many on spec
drafts and a great deal of unpaid time. Everything had to
be done according to stringent BBC guidelines, the first of
which was the required format in which all scripts must be
submitted. This alone took me several frustrating hours at
the computer to learn. I was deluged by the producers with
information about the programme which, far from being
a fiction, was as near to real life to those concerned with
making it as it was possible to be. Not only was I provided
with the names and backstories of every member of the permanent cast, but also with scale drawings of the fictional
doctors' group practice, complete with surgeries, reception
and waiting areas, where much of the drama was to unfold.
I realised quite early on that I was not only required to write
Episode 89 but to live it. Accustomed to being my own boss,
and unused to working either in a commercial or collaborative medium hedged about by accountants and 'suits', it
was one of the hardest and most soul-destroying tasks I had
undertaken, and it was to be a very long time indeed before
I would be set free.

My first step was to research 'battered baby syndrome', the
subject of 'my' episode that I had decided to call *Baby Blues*.
With a husband, four daughters and sons-in-law all in different professions, I had much of the information I needed on
tap, or at least at the end of a telephone. From my barrister
daughter, who had suggested the subject matter, I learned
the sad facts about the battered child syndrome, cases with
which, as a family lawyer, she was familiar. Battered child

syndrome referred to injuries sustained by a child as a result of physical abuse usually inflicted by an adult caregiver. Alternative terms for the condition included 'shaken baby', 'child abuse' and 'non-accidental trauma' for which internal injuries, cuts, burns, bruises and broken or fractured bones are all possible indicators. Contrary to belief, battered child syndrome was found at every level of society although the incidence was higher in low-income households where adult caregivers suffered greater stress and social difficulties, had often not had the benefits of higher education and in many cases had themselves been the victims of abuse. Although the children presented with anything from broken bones to burns and scald marks, establishing the diagnosis was often hindered by the excessive cautiousness of caregivers or the concealment of the true nature of the injuries as a result of fear, shame, or denial of what was actually taking place. Once the diagnosis had been made and the case came to the family court there was every chance that the judge would order the child to be removed from the mother or her surrogate and taken into care.

This tragic scenario was compounded, for the purposes of *Baby Blues,* by the fact that *osteogenesis imperfecta* or 'brittle bone disease' – a genetic disorder in which babies with congenitally fragile bones present with multiple fractures some of which may even have taken place in the womb – was sometimes misdiagnosed and mistaken for battered child syndrome (BCS). This misunderstanding, for which detailed research was necessary, formed the basis for my contribution to *Doctors.*

Some weeks later I produced the breakdown draft for 'Series 5 Episode 89' and sent it, as requested, to the script editor. After several more weeks of nail-biting, followed by many more attempts, draft *number thirteen* (each draft had gone through the same long-winded process) was accepted. The final breakdown for scene 22 of the episode looked like this:

EP89/SC22. INT. COURT. DAY. CONTINUED

CHERYL'S CASE WORKER gives evidence about how the baby came to be removed after a fresh injury yesterday, when the SS did not consider it a risk worth taking to leave the baby in the mother's care even for another 24 hours. She tells the JUDGE that just because the radiologist from St Phil's – who will give her evidence about the number and type of fractures sustained – has made the diagnosis of OI from the X-rays, it did *not* mean that CHERYL was a fit mother. Based on her observations of Cheryl with her baby on her visits to the family home, and of subsequent discussions with Cheryl, she has come to the conclusion that Cheryl has a volatile temper and that, furthermore, there is a family history of abuse by an alcoholic father which must also be taken into account.

Although I had put in a great deal of time and done countless hours of work, I still had not been paid. Finally however, in the due course of the BBC's time, the contract arrived. In addition to the basic (non-negotiable) fee, which at the time seemed not at all bad, an additional fifteen per cent for repeats was offered. At long last, and thinking I was now in the clear, I signed the agreement.

Having done much of the research into battered child syndrome, brittle bone disease, and family court procedure, having produced my scene-by-scene breakdown and had it approved by both the producer and script editor, I guessed that from now on *Baby Blues* would be plain sailing but the *Sturm und Drang*, that was to go on for the next six months (with rewrites required at short notice), had only just started.

Writers of soaps must bring a new and original voice to an existing milieu. This is hard for the novelist who is accustomed to creating a world of her own. While it is not necessary to have been an avid watcher of the programme, you have to like the already established characters and bring your voice-throwing skills as well as some new insight into their behaviour. While the series is formulaic, the medium demands that you should, at the same time, be original.

My story centred around an inadequate and depressed twenty-year-old single mother, Cheryl, who is suspected by the social services of maltreating her nine-month-old baby, Daisy, whose alleged brittle bone disease had been difficult to diagnose. Cheryl is terrified that the baby will be taken away from her and has been forbidden to be left alone with her daughter while the court case is pending. When Daisy screams with pain, for apparently no reason according to Cheryl, while her own mother is out of the room, the baby's grandmother can't help being suspicious. She suggests to Cheryl that they take the screaming baby to the Riverside surgery – run by Drs Mac McGuire, Helen Thompson and Georgina Woodson (the ongoing characters in the series). Cheryl is terrified when Dr Helen refuses to turn a blind eye to what she thinks might be Daisy's broken arm. Despite Cheryl's claims that she has done nothing to harm her baby and that she started crying spontaneously, the doctor is duty bound to alert the social services.

The Riverside doctors are divided about the pending court

case. To Dr George the case is clearly one of child abuse. Dr Helen, who knows Cheryl, who is treating her depression and will be called as a witness, has doubts. When Daisy, who yet again is diagnosed with a fracture, is kept in hospital under an Emergency Protection Order, Cheryl's hopes of the court deciding in her favour and of being allowed to keep her beloved baby fade.

As with any drama worth its salt, the play had to be driven not only by a plot but a subplot – or plots – which for the purposes of *Doctors* revolved around the members of the group practice themselves. Dr George consults Dr Helen about the progressive tremor she has been trying to conceal, which she has been keeping from her husband, the barrister representing Cheryl; Dr Helen thinks Dr George may be suffering from a life-threatening condition, which could be putting the patients at risk; the practice principal, Dr Mac McGuire, has problems with his convoluted love life.

A desperate Cheryl, despite evidence given by the suspicious social services who have brought the case, assures the court that she would never do anything to harm her baby, and a specialist in metabolic bone disease backs up her assertion that all Daisy's injuries are attributable to her brittle bone disease. There was, unfortunately, no definitive test for the well-documented condition, but his expert opinion was that it would be a grave mistake to suspect Cheryl of harming her child.

Having listened carefully to the evidence on both sides, the presiding judge praised the social services for carrying out their proper duties in protecting baby Daisy who was unable to protect herself and, thanking them for their astuteness, declared that they had 'every right to be suspicious'. While at this point Cheryl thinks she has lost her baby, the judge goes on to say that during the course of the proceedings he has heard absolutely nothing about Cheryl, other than that she has a quick temper, to convince him that she has abused Daisy. He orders the child to be returned to the care of her mother and dismisses the application for a Care Order.

While the 'story of the day', for which I was responsible, came to a happy conclusion and Cheryl and her baby would not be heard from again, Riverside and its practitioners had to go on. Dr George was anxiously awaiting the results of her blood tests, which would not be revealed until a later episode, Dr Mac's turbulent love life had yet to be resolved and, pending the next 'story of the day', for which thankfully I was not responsible, *Baby Blues* ended, like all good soaps, in the Lether bar, which the doctors frequented, on a cliffhanger.

Before a word of the above (apart from the scene-by-scene) was written, however, BBC protocol had to be followed. Firstly I had to assure the powers-that-be that I was not going to go away or be out of touch during the next three months over which my episode of *Doctors* was to be written. This was very inconvenient because we had a holiday booked – which we had to cancel – and it was not until later that I discovered the reason for this prohibition. Each one of my scenes had to be sent to the story editor, who would then show it to the producer, as it was written. Specific days on which they required the material were given to me. Being a very quick worker I saw this as no problem but every time I submitted a scene it came back accompanied by pages of comments. Not only did it have to incorporate a storyline of which I hadn't been told, but it had to be in front of the producer twenty-four (and sometimes as little as three) hours later. In the light of these deadlines I understood why I had not been allowed to leave the country.

Immobilised at my desk, I worked, often far into the night (when I am not at my writing best) to fulfil the stringent demands of the programme makers who had little idea of what they actually wanted and the drafts of scripts became like a series of dining options. First they fancied Indian, then Chinese, then Thai then – oh, what we *really* want is Indian after all! On one occasion I submitted work that was approved by the producer who soon afterwards quit her job (for reasons unknown to me), the result of which was that my episode of *Doctors* was put on hold while another producer for the programme was found. Naturally, the incoming producer had ideas of her own, which conflicted with those of her predecessor, leaving the exhausted writer back in square one. There was another stumbling block. Although I thought I had done my research thoroughly as far as the law court scenes, the social services and the medical side of things are concerned, nothing was taken for granted, in particular the laws of libel. While I held my breath in case yet another rewrite was demanded, the BBC's legal team was consulted on more than one occasion, their brief being to ensure that viewers would not be given grounds for protest. Despite the many, many frustrations for a writer who was used to being both her own editor and her own boss, I have to say that although the demands were overwhelming and fitted in neither with my writing nor my social life – which during the time I was producing Episode 89 of Series 5 of *Doctors* was put on hold – the resulting script was entertaining, accurate and thoroughly professional. But was it mine? A whole group of people had snatched it away from me, without so much as a thank you, and made what they could of it. Was it worth it?

Yes and no. While it was exhilarating to have contributed to a show loved by so many viewers, I had learned, the hard way, that the BBC was a fierce and unrelenting taskmaster, just how undervalued the writer is, and that when push came to shove I was capable of coming up with the goods immediately the penny was put into the slot. Always keen to extend my horizons, I now understood something about the ways of both barristers and the family courts, learned the pathology of previously unheard of diseases, followed the procedures of the understaffed social services, and managed to get an overall view of the workings of an up-to-date general medical practice.

The downside was that my long-established writing routine had been interrupted and, forced to burn the midnight oil I had been turned into a reluctant owl rather than a willing lark. I was tired to the point of exhaustion and both my desk and my family commitments were in disarray.

Would I do it again? Yes, if I was on the breadline; no, if I had the choice.

Having completed my script and had it finally approved, I had nothing further to do with the making of Episode 89, Scene 19 of which looked like this:

EP89/SC19.INT.COURT.DAY

RONNIE, DR EDWARD TROWBRIDGE
RONNIE:
What is your full name?
DR TROWBRIDGE:
My name is Edward Trowbridge and I am a Fellow of the Royal College of Physicians, a Fellow of the Royal College of Paediatricians, and a specialist in Metabolic Bone Disease at the Children's Royal Infirmary.

RONNIE:
Doctor Trowbridge, you have examined Daisy Westcott's X-rays. What is your opinion of them?
DR TROWBRIDGE:
I confirm the diagnosis of *Osteogenesis Imperfecta* …
RONNIE:
A disease which, as I am given to understand it, causes fractures in childhood.
DR TROWBRIDGE:
Precisely. Brittle Bone Disease is a disorder usually resulting from abnormalities in the genes that control production of a protein known as collagen. Collagen is the main protein in bone and is essential for its strength. Lack of collagen makes bones more vulnerable than normal and therefore they break more easily …
RONNIE:
The child would not then have to be *abnormally* handled?
DR TROWBRIDGE:
Absolutely not. Some children are born with fractures that take place *in the womb*. Some occur with normal handling and they can often be caused by the slightest touch.
RONNIE:
How did you arrive at your diagnosis?
DR TROWBRIDGE:
There is no specific test for *Osteogenesis Imperfecta*. The diagnosis is made on the basis of a number of characteristic features that may be found. I not only saw the X-rays but examined Daisy Westcott in person and carried out a Dexa Scan …
RONNIE:
Dexa Scan?

DR TROWBRIDGE:
To check bone density. On examination I also found a characteristic blueness in the whites of Daisy's eyes, although on its own this is not always a reliable indicator …
RONNIE:
In your expert opinion, would Daisy Westcott's injuries have been in any way consistent with abuse by the mother?
DR TROWBRIDGE:
Having *seen* Daisy Westcott, and having made the diagnosis of *Osteogenesis Imperfecta,* I think it would be a *grave mistake* to suspect Miss Westcott of harming her child …

The casting for Cheryl, her mother, and my other characters was carried out by the BBC and I was not invited to the shooting of the script. I forgot about *Doctors* and having taken a short and well-earned break, went back to my work and my orderly routine.

In the fullness of time I was sent a tape of Episode 89 and, before the actual programme went out, watched it with trepidation. They had done a wonderful job. Everything was as I had pictured it and no one was going to sue. It is reassuring to know that if ever I was to fall upon hard times I could always submit a few more ideas for the apparently never-ending series in the hope that at least one of them would be taken up.

11

Change of Heart

... He [Dickens] often used the play as a symbol of mortality itself.

PETER ACKROYD

After the debacle at the House of Stratus, I was left with no publisher for *Tsunami* and an as yet unstaged play, *Change of Heart*. If either the novel or the play were to be rescued from the recycle bin and see the light of day, something clearly had to be done. The will to persist, and the disinclination to waste a single crumb, is often strengthened and encouraged by the feedback one receives from 'fans' and the encouragement that comes from the knowledge that someone 'out there' is actually reading you. One such letter came at the appropriate moment from a lady in Worthing:

... Congratulations ... Your books are so warm, good stories – with such wit and humour that the characters are alive ... reading any other leaves me bored and disappointed, fail to keep my attention ... Many, many thanks for all the lovely hours of pleasure you have given me ... and happily more books to follow.

Tsunami, a powerful love story set in Paris, had started life as a film script (*Paris Summer*) cooked up by myself and my two film agents, Linda Seifert and Elizabeth Dench. Keen to write the seminal 'woman's movie' we met on a regular basis and thrashed out a scenario in which in the hottest summer in living memory, Judith Flatland, together with her two children, leaves Boston and her work at the Museum of Fine Arts, to follow her husband, Jordan, to Paris, where he is about to finalise a high-profile business deal. Bored with her role as 'corporate wife', conscious of her age, and suddenly aware that she has become sexually invisible, forty-two-year-old Judith feels jealous of and threatened by her nubile daughter and gets the impression that life is passing her by. Cheating on her marriage and unable to help herself, Judith is drawn into a passionate affair with a friend of her daughter's, Félix Dumoulin, a young artist. What begins as curiosity on her part and a bizarre wager on his, turns into a cataclysm as Judith is forced to choose between her husband and her lover.

The theme of the script was universal – we saw Meryl Streep as the protagonist – and had to do with jealousy, ageing, inequality between the sexes (more apparent then than now) and the maelstrom of emotions that torment women of a certain age. I had called the novel *Tsunami* because like those in the path of a tidal wave, Judith Flatland did not see her Armageddon coming and 'walked into it blind'.

Pleased with our script, which went from the snobbish heights of Boston's Beacon Hill to Parisian boulevards and the cemetery of Père Lachaise with its cat-infested tombs of Gustave Flaubert and Oscar Wilde, we sent it off to the studios and waited for the Hollywood greats to come knocking at our doors.

That the theme of our script was not a million miles away from my screenplay, *The Long Hot Summer*, which had come to within a whisker of getting made in Hollywood some years earlier, was unremarkable. When Picasso was asked why he was always to be found on the balcony painting the same view, he replied, 'Because every moment the light is different, the colours are different, the atmosphere is different.' Writers all have their niches and few completely escape from them.

When it was clear that despite enthusiastic but short-lived interest from Lifetime, the number one cable channel in the USA, *Paris Summer* was not going to get made – 'We love your script but we're shooting something very similar now with Michael Douglas', 'It would have to be shot in Paris and in today's economic climate that's too expensive'! – I set to work and once again, from the debris that invariably falls from every writer's table, my twentieth novel, *Tsunami* (which had been given such short shrift at House of Stratus by David Lane), found a publisher after a slew of rave rejections – 'As always I enjoyed Rosemary's writing but the market for fiction is increasingly competitive' – from the major publishing houses.

Having agreed to part company, albeit on amicable terms, with my agent, Sonia Land, it was my new agent, Heather Chalcroft, who placed *Tsunami* with gentleman publisher Robert Hale. But Hale did not go for the title, which 'no one will understand' (they would, of course, now), and we ended up with *Paris Summer* (as in the film script). Booker Prize-winner, the late Bernice Rubens, thought the novel 'a compelling and moving story' and gave her permission to be quoted on the jacket over a delightful and evocative painting, *Balcony Image*, by the artist Adrian George.

Although the novel was not widely reviewed – Robert Hale, while a respectable second eleven player, was not in the top echelon of publishers – it sold well to libraries and in no time at all the first printing was sold out. As usual the feedback from readers was gratifying: 'Lyrical, beautifully written, fascinating'; 'I read it in one sitting ... I can't believe how hooked I was'; 'A literary novel ... Deeply serious'; 'I read it late into the night and had to finish it'; 'It's such a wonderful book ... So true for everybody. I very much enjoyed it and read it in a day'; 'If ever a novel begged to be made into a movie it's this one ...'; 'I was reading until midnight'; 'I simply had to finish your book ... the clock struck 2 a.m. ... you kept me guessing to the end'; 'An absorbing book ... you needed time to sit back and savour all you'd read'; 'Had a wonderful sunny Paris day reading your book in the Palais Royal ... thoroughly enjoyed it ...'

As usual it was the readers, rather than the reviewers – in the case of *Paris Summer* conspicuous by their absence – who made the writer's life worthwhile and the fact that they once again found my work 'unputdownable' was deeply gratifying and all that an author could wish for. That *Paris Summer* started life as a screenplay may have accounted for the fact that a film producer from Los Angeles was 'crazy' about the book, could visualise its big screen potential and wanted permission to 'run with it' in LA. Needless to say, although permission was given, nothing came of her offer. Whether or not it was the fact that she had an injured shoulder at the time and needed major surgery followed by several months of therapy I shall never know. For all her 'running' there seemed no more mileage to be got out of *Tsunami/ Paris Summer* and I turned my attention elsewhere.

The one thing I had left in my cupboard was *Change of*

Heart. It was a good play with strong parts and a message that would raise the profile of the urgent need for organ donors. I dearly wanted to see it staged.

As with any play launched upon an uncaring world and in the good company of many major playwrights, the rejection rate was high. Since Jamie Barber, artistic director of the Yvonne Arnaud Theatre in Guildford, had both co-produced and successfully staged my first play *Home Truths*, he was first on the hit list but was busy at the time with his own agenda and did not want to know. True to form I was not downhearted, refused to take the rejections from a bunch of artistic directors personally, and regarded every rebuff as a fresh challenge. With plays, as with any work of art, it was horses for courses and I knew, from long experience, that every opinion was subjective and should never be regarded as the last word. The work of multimillionaire Damien Hirst, the renowned doyen of modern art, has been variously labelled by his detractors as 'decadent and worthless', 'of marginal interest', 'of little intrinsic value' and 'the last rattling breath of a world that has given up' while the man himself has been branded an 'artist who became a celebrity by pickling animals', accused of 'turning his name into a brand' and 'nicking one of his designs from a Smarties packet'. Hirst himself, I am sure, far from being gutted by his detractors, is laughing all the way to the bank.

A rehearsed reading of *Change of Heart* at the Soho Theatre set the wheels in motion for a full-scale production. At a 'rehearsed reading', a willing (and poorly paid) random cast of willing actors, previously provided with scripts of your play, sit in a semicircle on the stage before an invited audience of theatrical producers and directors who have nothing better to do with themselves, and as many friends and acquaintances you can rustle up and persuade to make their way to Soho on a rainy afternoon.

This reading, the first airing the play will have, gives the writer a chance to see if the script 'works', to judge the dramatic content and, most important of all, to find out if the interest of the audience will be held throughout and, if not, where the weaknesses of the script lie.

Apart from the fact that the actor (in this case a name well known from TV) who played Professor Jessie Sands (aka Professor Dame Julia Polak) was nursing an extremely bad cold, the exercise proved to be extremely useful. The feedback was gratifying and my sense that the play was nothing to be ashamed of and might have a future was reinforced. With no offers for an immediate West End production forthcoming but with the weak spots in the writing highlighted and the criticism taken on board, I went home, moderately pleased with myself, to write yet another draft. I had learned early on in my playwriting career that a play, like a piece of sculpture, is subject to change from the first tentative draft, through countless alterations and revisions, to the moment when first the director and then the actors superimpose their own input on the script. It is not necessarily a 'bad thing'. As long as everyone is working towards the same goal, i.e. the artistic and commercial success of the drama, and the writer retains the last word, all contributions are welcome.

After several more drafts, the merits of *Change of Heart* were recognised by Brian Daniels of the New End Theatre, Hampstead, who accepted it for production in his January 2004 programme. I was on my way. The sedate pleasure of seeing one of your novels in print cannot compare with the thrill of having a play produced. A book, no matter how successful, is launched into deafening silence and there is a distinct lack of applause. Although at this stage I had no idea that the final curtain of *Change of Heart* would leave me with a potentially fatal illness, the excitement generated by every stage of the production left me feeling almost equally ill.

While Brian Daniels, owner and artistic director of the New End Theatre, wanted to stage the play, investors had still to be found. A letter to potential benefactors read:

> We are presenting an important new play by writer Rosemary Friedman at the New End Theatre, Hampstead from 26th January 2004 for five weeks. The play *Change of Heart* is inspired by the true story of Julia Polak, Professor of Endocrine Pathology at Imperial College, London. Professor Polak was diagnosed in 1995 (at the age of 56) with one of the diseases she was studying – pulmonary hypertension. Only an urgent heart-lung transplant, performed by her eminent research colleague, Professor Sir Magdi Yacoub, saved her.

The letter went on to explain how the play examined the ethical implications of 'spare-part' surgery and the moral dilemmas of those (the surgeons) whose role it was to play 'God'.

While waiting for the potential backers to respond, a director – Annie Castledine, who had received a 'critics choice' award for her production of *All the Children Cried* at the West Yorkshire Playhouse – was approached and agreed to direct the play although, for a number of reasons, this proved to be a non-starter. Much time was wasted in abortive meetings and as far as *Change of Heart* was concerned we were back in square one. Michael Gieleta (his impressive CV revealed that he was fluent in English, Polish, Italian, French and Russian), whose work in the theatre ranged from *Lorenzaccio* to Strindberg and from the Royal Opera House to Chichester Festival Theatre, was hired to direct the play, which he did with considerable skill although we had the – not unusual – falling out at the end when I forgot my place and dared to instruct 'his' actors.

With the cast of six (including Julie-Kate Olivier) in place we were ready to go. Permission was sought from heart-transplant surgeon Professor Magdi Yacoub to portray him on stage and no objections were raised, although he did not know that in the play, in the guise of the Argentinian Professor Eduardo Cortes, he was required to dance a seductive tango. Rehearsals took place in the old Regent's Park Diorama building (later to be demolished) not a stone's throw from where I live and, treading on eggs as far as the easily ruffled feathers of Michael Gieleta were concerned, I managed to attend quite a few of them.

The play was due to open in January, not the kindest month of the year, and there were to be two gala evenings. The first of these was in aid of the Julia Polak Research Trust and the second was to benefit English PEN's Writers in Prison fund.

Lung disease, which included emphysema, chronic obliterative pulmonary disease, cystic fibrosis and pulmonary hypertension, was a major cause of death in the UK and a large-scale clinical problem. Until now the only sure way of addressing end-stage lung disease was transplantation from another person which would, with luck, provide the patient with ten to fifteen years of active life. The major drawbacks to this procedure were the chronic shortage of donor organs and the risk of rejection following transplantation. Researchers at the Imperial College Tissue Engineering Centre, led by Professor Polak, had made the important discovery of stem cells, which could be implanted to 'repair' lungs and avoid the need for transplantation. These new, functioning lung cells had been developed in such a way as to stop any chance rejection.

The two gala nights, one addressed by Julia herself and the other by the Chair of English PEN's Writers in Prison committee, were exciting and successful. The cast, playing to packed houses, rose to the occasions and, despite the filthy January weather, substantial funds were raised for both causes. Had I known what a downturn in my health the end of the run would bring, I doubt that I could have enjoyed the two evenings more. On the last night of the run, when the dreaded pantechnicon is stationed outside the theatre to transport the dismantled set to limbo-land, it is customary for the writer to show her appreciation to the loyal and hard-working cast. Feeling too sick with my oncoming illness to take them out to dinner, I visited their cramped dressing rooms to thank them for their efforts in making the play a success and presented them with souvenir teddy-bears wearing navy-blue sweaters on which was embroidered the name of the play, *Change of Heart*. I did not see the director, who was peeved with me for instructing the cast to make minor alterations in the final scene with which he did not agree, and after the hugging and the kissing and the statutory tears were over, took his teddy-bear home with me.

The reviews for *Change of Heart* were heartening. They ranged from 'this would make an intelligent choice for the West End', to ' … gripping play', '… this challenging human drama …' and '… this is dramatic gold'.

While West End producers were not exactly vying with each other for a transfer, an unanticipated approach from Houston, Texas, predicated what proved to be an entirely new ball game.

12

Deep in the Heart of Texas

Drama thrives on conflict ...

ARTHUR KOESTLER

Letter from Rebecca Greene Udden, Artistic Director at Main Street Theater, Houston, Texas, to my agent, July 2004:

Dear Ms Steinberg,

Main Street Theater, a professional non-profit theater in Houston, Texas, would like to produce Rosemary Friedman's play *Change of Heart*, for nine performances in November of 2004. The production dates will be Nov 3 (a preview performance) 4, 6, 7, 11, 12, 13, 14 and 19, a Gala fundraiser for Main Street Theater and a medical foundation. Main Street Theater is an Equity Theater (SPT level 2) and this production will be presented at the Chelsea Market Theater, which seats 200 people. Our ticket prices are $20 on Thursday nights, $25 on Friday nights and Sunday matinees, and $30 on Saturday nights. The preview tickets are $13. If you would like to know more about our company, our website is www.mainstreettheater.com. Please let me know what additional information you need from me in order to issue a licence for this production ...

This unexpected turn-up in July 2004, five months after the London production of *Change of Heart* came, like most good news, out of the blue. It had been facilitated by Denis Headon, the Director of the Texas/United Kingdom Collaborative Research Initiative at Rice University, who had been informed about the play by Julia. Rice University, which was underwriting the costs, was eager to raise funds for, and awareness of, heart-lung transplants and the desperate need for donors.

I had never been to Texas and had heard neither of Rice University nor Main Street Theater in Rice Village. Looking it up on the internet (what would we do without it?), I discovered that MST was a non-profit-making company dedicated to enriching the cultural lives of the community and which in addition to producing seminal plays from William Shakespeare to Alan Ayckbourn, had a thriving youth theatre.

Micheline, who was pleased as punch with the email she had received, sent a standard licence to perform the piece as requested, and made enquiries as to whether the university or the theatre was to pay my air fare and whether I would be able to attend rehearsals. In a prompt reply, Main Street Theater couldn't foresee any problems with either of these requests and emailed back: 'As soon as I know her travel needs we can get right on it.'

In August, I too received an email from Artistic Director Rebecca Udden:

> … I am very excited about the production and the resonances it will set up with our audiences, many of who work in the Texas Medical Center or in one of the nearby Universities. I am particularly excited by the dramatic strength of your play. … the story is compelling, interesting, and based on real events, but that doesn't always translate to a good

evening at the theater! ... Denis Headon, who brought the script to my attention, told me that you are contemplating making some changes in the script. ... we would want to start working on the production in September. Is that a reasonable time frame for you? I look forward to hearing from you and working on this project ...

Rebecca Udden also wanted to know whether Julie-Kate Olivier, who had played the lead in the London production of *Change of Heart*, would be willing and available to re-create the role in Houston. It was of course Julie-Kate's late father, Sir Laurence Olivier, which prompted her to ask for the name of her agent, rather than any rave reviews (sadly lacking) which Julie-Kate had received as the leading lady. We provided Houston with the information required.

Further communications, through Micheline, who with her eye to the main chance lost no time in introducing plays by other writers whom she represented to Main Street Theater, elicited the following response from Becky Udden:

... We have a fairly eclectic season and I am always looking for plays our audience won't have a chance to see elsewhere – neglected classics, women playwrights, new works. My interests are wide-ranging but I prefer articulate, challenging plays to single issue or topical plays. I'll have to confess to a fundamental optimism which often steers me away from plays that require me to spend an evening with hateful people doing hateful things to each other and learning nothing from it ...

She confirmed that Business Class air tickets would be made available for both myself and my husband and that our entire stay in Houston was to be 'hosted' (i.e. paid for) by the Warwick Hotel.

The future looked rosy. With a song in my heart and unable to believe my luck I started on the rewrites of the play for the American market. Unlike a novel, a play grows and changes, both in rehearsal and on stage and in the mind of the author. Trying not to let the heady days of summer distract me, I worked like fury and finally pressed the save button on *Change of Heart*: 'Final Draft Texas 2004'.

While details of rehearsals: '… Saturday through Thursday evenings, Friday off first two weeks … tech rehearsals … dress rehearsals … and performances. (No performances Saturday, November 5th … Gala Performance Friday November 19th …)' flew back and forth, the cheque, which would secure the licence for the play, was, true to form, slow in arriving. '… I've been out of the office all week … It's the end of our fiscal year and we had to wait for a grant to come in … The bookkeeper is only in on Tuesday … Sorry it has taken so long … August is our really slooow month!'

While in Houston August was a 'really slooow month', life in the UK for Micheline and other theatrical agents was hectic. Micheline to Rebecca: '… Our August is often frantic with the Edinburgh Festival and new plays scheduled for the autumn/spring seasons. … When you forward the cheque would you mind also enclosing copy of signed licence … PS I shall be away from the office Friday until Monday inclusive.'

While the two women fought it out, Julie-Kate Olivier, in receipt of the offer to go to Texas via her agent, was tickled pink. She would sort out her plans for November. The good news was that monies and the licence to perform the play finally arrived from Main Street but: '… we are unable to pay you until the cheque has cleared sterling in our account. Best wishes, Micheline.'

The bad news was that by October 2004 Main Street Theater seemed suddenly to have gone off the radar. At the end of August their computer had crashed and they were incommunicado until the second week in September when much to my relief they came back on track. I was informed about travel plans by the delightfully named Shannon Emerick de los Reyes (Rebecca Udden – Becky's – assistant) who confirmed that Continental Airlines had generously agreed to sponsor my First Class ticket to Houston.

Julia Polak was delighted with the ongoing arrangements for the Houston production of *Change of Heart* and in particular with the fund-raising spin-off, which would benefit the Trust and raise significant amounts of money for joint research projects. I was delighted to be the catalyst for all this. In an email to all concerned Julia stated that Lord Sainsbury, as Minister of Science and in conjunction with the DTI, had set up, together with key people at various universities of Texas, an agreement to collaborate by supporting scientists to travel to the UK and vice versa. They would also discuss potential research projects that would bring in larger funding from the NIH and other government bodies. The idea was to *collaborate*, *create* and *commercialise* and to stimulate the exchange of ideas. Tissue Engineering and Stem Cells was one of the most successful areas of this collaboration and the intention was to set up other groups who would work together to attract larger funding. The Presidents of each of the Texas universities had contributed to the scheme and the man in overall charge was Denis Headon, who was eagerly awaiting a visit by President George W. Bush to his Heart Medical Center.

My reworked script (geared to a transatlantic audience) having been delivered to Main Street, airline tickets having been secured and the invitation to stay at the Warwick Hotel having been accepted, I informed all my friends in the US, from New York to Chicago and San Francisco, who were waiting to book their tickets to see the show, of the final arrangements.

At the end of September, I was flabbergasted to hear from Denis Headon that the run of another author's play, *Some Mother's Sons,* had already been tentatively booked by MST for November 2004 and that it was unable to be rescheduled. MST were now suggesting that *Change of Heart* should have one special performance on 28 February or 1 March 2005 – when Julia and Professor Magdi Yacoub would be in Houston for a stem cell meeting – and that this should be followed by staged performances at the Main Street Theater in the fall of that year. Further to this confusing email he would call me the following day. Which he did.

Although I was disappointed not to be going to Texas in 2004 as I had thought (and excitedly announced to everyone), the ebullient Shannon de los Reyes seemed not discombobulated by the proposed rescheduling: 'Hello, Ms Friedman! I hear there's been good news and that you'll be visiting us at a different time of year! I will await your travel dates and then will get back in touch with Continental …'

On 7 October 2004, when my US friends had already booked their flights and I should by rights have been getting ready for my trip to Texas, Denis Headon expressed his concern about the turn events had taken to Julia, suggesting she call him asap. He also wrote to Main Street Theater, with a carbon copy to myself:

I am meeting with Gwin Morris* at 2.00pm today regarding the possibility of fund-raising at the Gala Performance – I shall respond to you all after the meeting. In Julia's email of last week she indicated that she and Rosemary had talked and agreed that a full staging of the play in your 2005–6 season would be the preferable option as Julia can return for the Gala ...

There followed emails from Rebecca Udden to Denis Headon, and Denis Headon to Rebecca Udden:

Hello Denis,

This production has taken on a life of its own totally outside Main Street Theater, and I am struggling to find my place in the process! Let me affirm that I like the play very much and think it will resonate with our audiences. But next year's season has not begun to take shape and it won't for a while. I am sorry to inconvenience anyone but I have to make programming decisions based on what I think will be best for the company and that takes time. It WILL make it easier to decide to produce the play if we have a firm commitment from Dr Morris (or someone) not only to provide underwriting but to partner with us in getting the attention we need in the community to attract the audience that I feel is there for the play ... I know this is a very important project to you, Denis, and you have put a lot of effort into coordinating it. The bottom line for us though, is that it will be expensive and will require more staff time than usual. I'm

_____

* Vice President for Public Affairs at the University of Texas Health Science Center in Houston

not sure if everyone involved understands just how small our staff is or even how this project came about. Initially, the production was to be a special project with a medical center partner whose participation would ensure that the production would benefit Main Street in a financial as well as an artistic way. When we really couldn't get that commitment from anyone, we had to cancel the plans for November. We are already struggling with a deficit from the past two years. I am hopeful that this can still work, but I don't want anyone to think it's just a matter of picking a date to mount a production ...

Dear Becky,

... please be assured that I see your position as central in the process. I am just back from my meeting with Dr Morris and he feels that a Gala Performance can raise money for all concerned but that the main beneficiaries would have to be medical research as the mission of his development office is exactly that. It would be impossible for him to use members of his development board and his staff to raise the funds for the Gala and not have most of these funds go to medical research. I guess that the message was we all – UTHSC-Houston, Julia Polak Research Trust and Main Street Theater – need to get their expectations from a Gala Performance in sync. While I fully understand that planning for your next season has not yet commenced I do have a concern that if MST take a long time to reach a decision, and if that decision is not to stage *Change of Heart* it will leave little opportunity to try to make some alternative arrangements and this great opportunity will be lost. When would MST normally decide on its 2005–6 season?

Rebecca Udden to Micheline Steinberg, 29 October 2004:

Dear Micheline,

We are considering the show for the coming season and the likeliest time will be the January–February time period. Generally I begin trying to put the next year's season together in January. Right now the theater is going through some major organizational re-structuring which will offer some new challenges and which are taking all my attention …

From Micheline Steinberg to Rosemary Friedman:

Subject: Play. To be or not to be …

I do think that this is for the best but it has been a very messy affair and will need more planning …

Like a rabbit caught in the glare of the headlights, I began to feel distinctly uncomfortable and hoped that the fear which had begun to niggle in my cerebral cortex would not prove to be justified.

While Denis Headon, Rebecca Udden and Micheline Steinberg slugged it out between them Julia, as is her wont, although unversed in theatric protocol, remained optimistic: '… had a long chat with Denis. We both feel that the best course of action would be to have a PROPER Gala night when the play is on: September/October (2005!). I will keep you posted.'

And subsequently, in April 2005 when hopes for a Houston production of *Change of Heart* were dwindling rapidly:

I suggest the following: 1. Keep pestering Denis. 2. Keep in touch with Suzie Lanie, PA of James Willerson who has the contacts. Telephone call? 3. Contact the administrator of Rice University. He may suggest other venues. 4. Keep in contact with Dr Morris. OK? Keep me posted.

It was all very well for Julia. She may have been the bee's knees as far as heart-lung transplants and tissue engineering were concerned, but she knew next to nothing about the ways of the theatrical world. As hopes for the USA premiere of *Change of Heart* faded, I reconciled myself to the fact that it had been nothing but a nail-biting chimera and, unaware that chemotherapy rather than a putative Houston production of my play would occupy me in the autumn of 2005, I picked up the pieces of my life.

While, having had my hopes raised and (to my embarrassment) having urged my friends in the USA to book their tickets to Houston, I was extremely disappointed, I was not downhearted. Of course it would have been nice to visit Texas (we had planned to travel around during the proposed run of the play), of course being the catalyst for worthwhile raising of funds for tissue engineering would have been gratifying, but if you can't stand the heat you don't stay in what is the writer's metaphorical kitchen.

While leaving *Change of Heart* on a back burner for the time being, I put on my metaphorical apron, opened my metaphorical recipe book, picked up my metaphorical wooden spoon and began work on the next metaphorical meal.

13

My Grandmother's Chicken Soup

Tell me what you eat, and I'll tell you who you are ...
JEAN ANTHELME BRILLAT-SAVARIN

My interest in cooking began in childhood when I learned from my maternal grandmother how to make a perfect chocolate mousse. The recipe for this has now been entrusted to my second daughter who for high days and holidays, when the extended family gathers for celebration, turns it out to perfection:

Ingredients:
1 egg per person plus an extra white
1 oz of chocolate per person
1 oz of caster sugar per person

It's as simple as that. On the surface. The skill is in the preparation and it doesn't need a Heston Blumenthal with his culinary laboratory, his 'sound of the sea' razor clams on a bed of tapioca, his frog blancmange, his snail porridge and his bone-marrow (!) rice pudding to turn out a mousse smooth as silk in consistency, satisfyingly chocolatey to the taste and beloved by all. It was my late mother-in-law who taught me that the secret ingredient of the successful cook was neither difficult to obtain nor expensive to come by. It was love! As with writing, at least with writing that anybody wants to read, you have to cook with your entire being, to involve each one of your five senses, to touch and feel and smell as if you were distilling a rare perfume, smoothing and refining a beautiful jewel. If not, don't bother. Pick up a 'ready meal', switch on the TV, satisfy the hunger and forget about hitting the spot that will fix the dish in your memory as surely as a good book or an exquisite piece of music.

Following the verbal instructions – they have never been written, only handed down – for the family chocolate mousse is only part of it.

Whip the yolks with the sugar.

Sounds easy. My grandmother in her kitchen with its free-standing enamelled gas cooker and oil-cloth-covered table, used a wooden spoon in an heirloom cream-glazed stoneware Mason Cash bowl and what must have been an extremely strong right arm to whip to the exact point where the pallid mixture could hold patterns when traced with a spoon. It could sometimes take her half an hour to do what today's food processors can do in minutes. But she was not in a hurry: she did not write books although I am sure, given the opportunities that women have today, she could have masterminded a business if not run a bank, removed an appendix or captured the Falklands.

Melt the chocolate.

A heat-proof bowl in the then ubiquitous Pyrex ware made of shatterproof lantern glass (I still have a few pieces left, which today are probably collectors' items), placed over an aluminium pan of boiling water held a slab of Bourne-ville chocolate snapped into its marked-out squares. Today there are other options, chocolate from France and Belgium, from Italy, Ecuador and Venezuela: Green & Black's and Montezuma's, Bernard Castelain and Valrhona, purest dark chocolate loaded with flavonoids – antioxidant chemicals including catechins and phenols that help prevent cell damage, reduce clot formation and improve blood-sugar levels – suggesting that in the not too distant future it will be available on prescription.

The temperature of the bowl is of the essence. Too cold and the squares will remain obstinately square-shaped. Too hot – letting the water in the pan boil – will result in a dull and solidified mass. The secret is NOT TO STIR IT: to turn the gas off when the water has reached boiling point enabling the chocolate to melt voluptuously into a thick dark liquid, smooth and shining and ready to pour in a molten stream into the beaten yolks.

Whip the egg whites.

A doddle with the electric-powered Kenwood with its plethora of attachments, which will whisk and beat and chop and grate and liquidise at will. My grandmother used a rotary beater, which must be turned by a strong right hand until, in what seemed to my childish eyes a culinary miracle, the pale puddle of viscous liquid quadrupled its volume and overflowed the bowl in a billowy cloud of firm and snowy peaks.

With no stamped-on lions or other indication of freshness, the eggs were sometimes dodgy and had to be discarded. One by one my grandmother broke them into a saucer ('what's a saucer, Granny?') which she then held to her nose. It was a useful tool. In the absence of a 'sell-by date' – how she would have laughed – it indicated when to discard the leftovers in her antediluvian fridge, when the butter was 'off' and when the milk was sour. It was hard work. The knife blades in her kitchen were polished with pink 'knife paste' and the mud-caked vegetables cleaned and chopped by hand. When she wanted 'mince' for her meat loaf in which a hard-boiled egg appeared miraculously in the middle, or her shepherd's pie (which would last the week) with the adroitness of a metalworker she assembled a heavy, cast-iron mincer with its rubber feet, wing nut, and detachable blades with different-gauge holes, which must be clamped on to the table before its wooden handle was laboriously hand cranked.

I was trained, at cookery school, to separate the eggs in the palm of my hand allowing the whites to slither through my fingers, to rub the mixing-bowl with lemon (to remove any vestige of grease) and to add a pinch of salt when whipping the whites. My grandmother had no need of the Cordon Bleu bible, its recipes set in stone. Today's influential chefs, the foul-mouthed gods and seductive goddesses of the popular TV programmes, would have been laughed out of court. In her kitchen my grandmother, like the writer, 'knew' because she 'knew'. Scorning the cumbersome scales, with their circular weights, from 1lb to 1oz, in diminishing circles, on baking day, she threw in a bit of this and a bit of that using her eyes and her hands and did not need to be told, at the end stage of her chocolate mousse, to take infinite care when gently folding the beaten whites into the whipped yolks and to trace a figure of eight in the bowl with a metal spoon.

The highlight of my day of course, when the mixture had been poured into Woolworth's best crystal, was to scrape the ambrosial chocolate residue – my version of Proust's 'madeleine' – from the sides of the bowl. The younger members of my family still vie for the honour when the mousse has been served up and, to the uninitiated, scarcely a spoonful remains.

'When from a long distant past nothing subsists, after the people are dead, after the things are broken and scattered, still, alone, more fragile, but with more vitality, more unsubstantial, more persistent, more faithful, the smell and taste of things remain poised for a long time, like souls, ready to remind us ...' Proust's *Rememberance of Things Past* and recent psychoanalytic theory suggest that eating practices are essential to self-identity and are instrumental in defining family, class and even ethnic identity. Food and related imagery have long been part of literature. From Chaucer's *Canterbury Tales*, through Ernest Hemingway with his '... oysters with their strong taste of the sea and their faint metallic taste ...' to Margaret Atwood who uses food and eating disorders to address issues of gender, language and sexual politics, it has been used for inspiration, plot device and as a method of revealing character. In my 1987 novel *To Live in Peace* I include recipes for fresh-water carp and 'tzimmes' (glazed carrots) and honey-cake in Kitty Shelton's letters from New York to her daughter, Rachel.

Together with John Steinbeck I regard the ubiquitous 'chicken soup' as a culinary *sine qua non*. Using age as my justification, I have all but given up on this particular task, which requires both time and physical strength (to lift the heavy pan) and again leave it to my daughters who even in middle age have not quite mastered the skill.

In his 1952 novel *East of Eden,* Steinbeck pre-empts the day when the curative powers of chicken soup – acknowledged in the twelfth century by Maimonides who strongly recommended it for people suffering from haemorrhoids and the early stages of leprosy – would be recognised and it would be known throughout the world as 'Jewish penicillin': 'And Tom brought him chicken soup until he wanted to kill him. The lore has not died out of the world, and will still find people who believe that soup will cure any hurt or illness and is no bad thing to have for a funeral either.'

On paper, chicken soup is a broth made by 'boiling chicken parts or bones in water, with various vegetables and flavourings'. This is tantamount to saying that *War and Peace* is no more than a text concocted by sprinkling several hundred suitably sized pages with a variety of printed words arranged in uniform lines and sticking them together.

As far as my early days in the kitchen were concerned the 'chicken soup saga' began in the early mornings before the family was awake. Like writing, for which according to Kafka 'one can never be alone enough', silence and solitude were the two key ingredients: they concentrated the mind. In the old days, in the Jewish kitchen, the chicken, which arrived with a full complement of giblets, had to be 'koshered' – soaked and salted – according to biblical injunction. Today, of course, it is obtained pre-packed and ostensibly, although I always give it a good wash, ready for the pot which in my grandmother's day – I still have it in my attic – was gross and black and big enough to bath a baby in, acknowledging the unwritten rule that you can never make too much chicken soup or too many roast potatoes. Covering the bird, and at least three accompanying sets of giblets and a meat bone or two if one is no purist, with cold water, one sets it on a low gas until it comes to the boil at which point the 'make or break time' has arrived. The reaction of the boiling water with the chicken will produce a thick foam or 'scum', which rises to the top of the saucepan and must be gently and meticulously removed with a metal spoon and then discarded. A small amount of salt together with approximately another third of a pint of cold water is then added and the pot is watched *sans interruption* until once again the water boils when the procedure is repeated. This time-consuming ritual, repeated until no further scum rises to the surface, needs the patience of a saint, the skill of a surgeon and the eyes of a hawk. Failure to carry it out correctly will result in not the crystal-clear and golden traditional broth but in a saucepan full of a muddy and opaque liquid, which is pleasing neither to eye nor tongue.

The 'skimming', which often takes place over a span of thirty minutes, is followed by a lowering of the heat and the introduction of the vegetables and seasonings, which will give the soup its distinctive flavour. The choice of vegetables is idiosyncratic, but there should be a copious amount of them. My grandmother used to swear by something called 'root' – a cross between a carrot and a turnip – which I believe originated in Eastern Europe and today has faded into oblivion. Leek, celery, carrot, turnip, parsnip, swede, parsley and courgette, cut into pieces, are some of the possibilities, every cook having her favourite selection. With the addition of flavourings, salt and white pepper and a few threads of genuine saffron soaked for a while in a small quantity of boiling water – some swear by the magical powers of a sugar cube – the preparation is complete and the soup is left to simmer infinitesimally gently, preferably for eight hours by which time it will have transmogrified into a translucent and golden liquid, which pervades not only the kitchen but the entire house with a fragrance guaranteed to stimulate a remembrance of things past. Some three hours into this time, according to the age of the bird, the chicken is removed from the broth, the meat taken from the bones (it should fall off) later to be disguised with a tasty sauce for the table, and the carcass returned to the saucepan.

This is not all. When the cooking, which is preferably carried out a day before the soup is needed, has been done and the contents of the saucepan cooled, it must be strained into a clean bowl through a fine-meshed sieve, the by now flaccid vegetables discarded and the giblets, for those with enough stomach to fancy them, added to the broth. When the bowl is cool enough it is put into the fridge where by the following day, with a bit of luck, it will have turned into a fragrant jelly and the fat solidified into a rich layer on the top. This must be carefully removed with a slotted spoon and discarded or used for frying or baking according to your views on the undesirability of hydrogenated fats. Any small beads of residue idling on the surface may be soaked up using kitchen paper.

The soup, while now ready, is not yet complete. The addition of 'matzoh balls' – matzoh meal, beaten egg, more chicken fat and water – rolled out with wetted hands and solid as bullets or ethereal as gossamer, according to your skill, is mandatory. Some swear by the addition of vermicelli, others will add fresh vegetables or shreds of exhausted chicken meat while the soup is gently reheated. Watch it like a hawk: let the cauldron boil at your peril. If you turn your back the soup will lose its translucence, which can never be restored.

It is a two-day job. Is the Herculean effort that goes into the preparation of what, at the end of the day, is no more nor less than a bowl of soup, worth it? Every day, when one has better things to do – no. Once or twice a year when the family is expectantly assembled – yes. Eating is a fundamental human activity that is necessary not only for survival but is inextricably connected with social function. Eating habits, the choice of companions and the reasons behind these choices are fundamental to fostering an understanding of human society. Dining rituals provide a framework that directly reflects and expresses human desires and behaviour.

When I think that in my long and blessed lifetime I have cooked so many thousands of meals I surprise myself. Times, of course, have changed. In my childhood and early marriage, it was three meals a day with feet under the table. In middle-class homes, while many of the underprivileged went hungry, three courses at lunch and dinner were de rigueur. Standing at the stove, in between my writing and in blissful ignorance of today's ubiquitous diets and calorie counts, I produced killer roasts and casseroles, grills and fry-ups and always a home-made pudding, treacle or trifle, jellies and custards. Today all that the heart – or the stomach – desires is pre-cooked meals and I don't know if it's my imagination or if they really taste of nothing so much as the brightly coloured box they come in. I would not wish the 'old' days back. First, I no longer have the physical strength that my grandmother, even in old age, never seemed to lose; second, I have better and more productive things to do. On family occasions, however, when I look round my well-filled dining table, when I politely declare my daughters' culinary efforts superior to my own, I wonder whether we have locked the door on a heritage informed by culinary tradition and thrown away the key. While the French have their frog's legs and their cassoulet, the Italians their pasta, the Germans their Tafelspitz, the Bangladeshis their rice, the Hungarians their goulash, the Pakistanis their chapattis and the Indians their sambas and rasams, will my own occasional efforts – efforts being the operative word – to perpetuate my grandmother's chicken soup preserve, for a generation at least, my own past?

14

The Dinner Party Book

Vera adored arranging things, be it a party with punch, a visa or a wedding.

VLADIMIR NABOKOV

Every publication of a book provides the *raison d'être* for a party, not that I really need an excuse. Like Vera Nabokov I love arranging things and whether it be 'a party with punch, a visa or a wedding' or in my case a new book, the first night of a play, a wedding, a landmark birthday or an anniversary, a substantial amount of time, energy and attention to detail goes into it. While for the *über*-intellectual Simone de Beauvoir the effort of turning your house into a palace and yourself into a queen is only to be regarded with the contumely it deserves, I must confess I like it, although sometimes, afterwards, when the guests have departed, the money has been spent and the moment is past I wonder whether, in the grand order of things it was really worth it.

It starts very small. Many months in advance and with the idea of an idea. A date is selected, preferably a Thursday, which is usually the day of the week most publishers prefer to launch a book, and the guest list, like the outline of a novel, sketched in. Once pen, or pencil has been put to paper – at this early stage the computer does not come into play – the planned celebration takes on a life of its own and there is no going back.

A reception involves something more than merely welcoming others into a woman's home; it changes this dwelling into a domain of enchantment; the social function is at once a party and a ceremony. The hostess displays her treasures: silver, linen, glassware; she arranges cut flowers. Ephemeral and useless, flowers typify the needless extravagance of parties marked by expense and luxury; open in their vases, doomed to early death, they take the place of bonfires, incense and myrrh, libations, offerings ...

The woman who presides over these mysteries, according to the supercilious Madame de Beauvoir: '... is proud to feel herself the creator of a perfect moment, the bestower of happiness and gaiety. It is through her that the guests have been brought together, an event has taken place; she is the gratuitous source of joy and harmony.'

These sentiments are echoed by Virginia Woolf's Mrs Dalloway:

But suppose Peter said to her, 'Yes, yes, but your parties – what's the sense of your parties?' all she could say was (and nobody could be expected to understand): They're an offering ... Here was So-and-so in South Kensington; some one up in Bayswater; and somebody else, say in Mayfair. And she felt quite continuously a sense of their existence; and she felt what a waste; and she felt what a pity; and she felt if only they could be brought together; so she did it. And it was an offering to combine, to create, but to whom? An offering for the sake of an offering, perhaps. Anyhow it was her gift. Nothing else had she … Anybody could do it; yet this anybody she did a little admire, couldn't help feeling that she had, anyhow, made this happen.

If there is pure generosity in this service rendered to others, the party is truly a party, but if the party becomes a social routine, a tit-for-tat occasion, when old scores are settled, it quickly changes celebration into institution, gift into obligation and elevates the occasion to the status of a rite. A rite, in common with many, I perpetuated in the early days of my marriage when, as a young bride, I was new to the 'social scene' and had just set up home.

It started with the 'dinner party book', given to me by my sister as a birthday present and which I still keep, albeit in an up-to-date form, unto this day. A claret-coloured, leather-bound volume the pages of which are blank save for 'Luncheon/Dinner', 'Date', 'Guests', 'Menu/Wines', 'Flowers', 'Gown and Jewels Worn' and 'Notes', on the left-hand side, and a table plan waiting to be filled in on the right! I blush to think that a lifetime ago I actually filled in all the sections under the requisite headings, although today, the dinner party book is an eloquent document and testament to the times which, since I first set out my 'festive articles' – 'glassware' and 'tablecloth' 'champagne and sweets' – have long passed.

What hard work 'entertaining' was! Although it was a far cry from Mrs Dalloway's 'grand deception': '… with a wave of the hand … the table spreads itself voluntarily with glass and silver, little mats …' on which '… films of brown cream mask turbot …' and '… in casseroles severed chickens swim'. Those early dinner parties, each meticulously recorded in the gold-embossed book, a social document for posterity, were not a million miles away.

From where I stand now, unable and unwilling to put more than a one-course meal on the kitchen table, to walk more than a short distance or remove the lid from a screw-top jar without the aid of a 'gadget' – in the same way as I am unable to give credence to the fact that I raised four children with their physical and emotional needs and at the same time wrote books and helped my husband who in the early days of our marriage, before he became a psychiatrist, was in general medical practice – I can't believe how I did it. Perhaps I should have paid more attention to Horace and 'seized the day' but then I was too busy. Or was it too stupid? Do we ever appreciate anything at the time? One just gets on with it.

The first 'modest' entry in the dinner party book is Sunday Night Supper for seven people! It seems hardly worth it. The menu consisted of 2 chickens, 1 tongue (how could we?!), 2 lb of hot dogs, 12 stuffed eggs, 12 stuffed tomatoes, Golden Rice Salad, ratatouille (v. popular), green salad, orange water-ice, fresh orange salad and the ubiquitous chocolate mousse which, in what appears to be a deviation from the norm, a variation on a theme, appeared to have consisted of 9 eggs, 15 oz of chocolate and 9 oz of sugar. Needless to say, everything – except of course the hot dogs – was cooked at length and at home. The ox tongue, large and pink and pickled in brine, was boiled until tender, placed on a dish and for twenty-four hours or overnight, weighted down, for some unfathomable reason, with the heaviest tins from the larder (what's a larder, Granny?) one could find. The chickens, barely fitting into the newly-weds' New World, free-standing gas cooker, were routinely roasted, the dozen tomatoes and dozen hard-boiled eggs painstakingly stuffed at the Easiwork, pull-down table, the tomatoes with chicken liver for which fresh chicken livers had to be grilled for two minutes (to remove the blood) and afterwards fried in chicken fat with onions and put through the mincer, a pale replica of my grandmother's. The Golden Rice Salad, studded with green and red pimento, and the ratatouille, a mouth-watering mélange of tomatoes and onions and peppers and aubergine flavoured with spices, cooked and served in an appropriate dish: china white to show off the rich red vegetables to advantage or silver because it was a wedding gift, and you had it. The green salad had to be divested of its earth clods and its bugs (several changes of salt water) – none of your vacuum-packed bags of multifarious leaves in those days – the orange water-ice removed from the inadequate ice-making compartment of the fridge and churned at appropriate intervals and the chocolate mousse lovingly fabricated and decanted into its cut-glass bowl. It makes me tired now even to think of it. Whatever help I had in the guise of weekly visits from a loquacious cleaner and the ubiquitous au pair who 'helped' with the children when the mood so took her and she wasn't weeping over a doomed love affair or washing her hair or clutching a hot-water bottle (what's a hot-water bottle, Granny?) to her belly to assuage her seemingly perpetual period pains, was insignificant when compared with my own labours in the kitchen for which I suffered, being a perfectionist, and to which, as when writing a novel, I gave my undivided attention and expected no less than one hundred per cent perfect results.

O tempora, o mores! What I could only have done with that time. But could I? The Sunday Supper guest list consisted of Carmel Ross, sister of Aubrey (later Abba) Eban, Israel's Foreign Minister from 1966 to 1974, the late György (George) Faludy, poet, writer, translator and celebrated author of *My Happy Days in Hell,* an account of his life in a Hungarian labour camp, two cousins – he a former senior civil servant in Nairobi and she an erstwhile actress – my sister and brother-in-law and the prize-winning novelist Gerda Charles (née Edna Lipson) with whom I was later to fall out and who has since died. Did they appreciate the two-day cooking *Fest* which had preceded the pretentious 'buffet'? I doubt it. As far as I was concerned despite the planning and the cooking and the work involved in creating the *mise en scène,* like a well-honed short story or a chapter in a novel it was a job well done. Subsequent dinner parties took excess, in terms of time and effort, even further although, because everyone in our social circle was doing it in an ongoing game of musical dining chairs, it did not seem so then. Leafing through the dinner party book I see that the exotic contents of the menus continued on a meteoric rise: *consommé madrilène* (in itself a day's work), *caneton* (4 ducks!) *aux cerises, paella* with green salad, *crêpes pralinés* with *kissell* (a mixture of red summer fruits, their juices thickened with cornflour), mushroom vol-au-vents (how that dates one), beef olives, chicken Marengo (something to do with Napoleon), pâté maison and pears in red wine.

If the food was ambitious, the wines were even more so. Donated by my husband's grateful patients at Christmastime, they would fetch fortunes today: Château Haut-Marbuzet (1961), Château Latour (1963), Puligny Montrachet (1987) and Piper Heidseck champagne. According to my records our 'French Country' dining table with its hideous caned chairs, which could tell a story or two and which is still in occasional service today, held 'red garnet roses and madeira mats', 'daffodils on a yellow tablecloth', 'pink tulips and matching candles', 'primroses in a green vase'.

Over the years, according to my 'bible', we entertained friends and family, writers and politicians, agents and publishers, actors and musicians. Little did they know that their entries in the 'book' were followed (in brackets) by acid remarks such as 'no show' or 'boring', 'turned up late' or 'too rude to reply'. If the names of the guests were inscribed for all time, so too was my 'wardrobe'. Under 'Gowns and Jewels Worn' I see 'green silk skirt and ribbed top', 'rose-patterned trousers', 'black dress with gold spots' and 'velvet skirt with yellow shirt'. I can't even remember them now but I suspect that today they might fetch a good price in a vintage shop. If the food and the clothes, seen through the wrong end of the telescope, were bizarre, my comments under 'Notes' were even more so: 'all very good and much appreciated', 'double the fish recipe', 'X never stops talking' and 'Y is too quiet', 'wrong guests for this menu', 'v. successful but a lot of work', 'worth repeating', 'keeps hot well', 'pâté slightly salty' and 'Alfred likes potatoes'. All this entertaining was probably facilitated by the fact that unlike today, when, like Banquo's ghost they have no qualms about appearing at your dinner party, watch TV till all hours, rely on parental help with their homework, engage in dialectic and are up till all hours, children, unbelievably, not only went to bed but went to sleep at six!

Interspersed with these dinners – how stuffy they were compared with the informal gatherings of today when kedgeree, a fish pie, or half a dozen dishes from the Lebanese takeaway (hummous, taramasalata, babaganoush) will suffice – were the publication parties of which to date, between us – my husband started writing in his seventies – there have been twenty-five. No matter how short of space we are, we always have them at home where the mixture of friends and family, publishers, agents, playwrights and novelists, editors, sales reps and PR girls fresh from their Eng. Lit. courses, seems to gel. One very important fallout from the publication party held at home is that it sells books. Having accepted your hospitality, it would be a churlish guest who would not take home a signed copy of your new book sold at trade price. In the absence of a vast publicity spend, in these days a rarity, your new baby will be launched, with a bit of luck and provided you have done your job well, with the best of all promotion, 'word of mouth'. The effectiveness of this is well documented and even better known. How often have we said to friends 'you must read this book/go to that play/see this film'? In an exponential curve they will, it is hoped, pass on the recommendation to their friends and acquaintances, and their friends and acquaintances to theirs and there you go. For the price of a few glasses of moderately decent (wine club) wine and sufficient canapés (catered) to make dinner a matter of choice rather than necessity, useful networking is carried out, friendships are cemented and your book is launched.

Although many well-known and literary figures have passed through our doors, I would not label these evenings 'literary'. In common with Sir Terry Pratchett, with whom I once served on the committee of the Society of Authors and who is now unfortunately a victim of Alzheimer's disease, a diagnosis which every writer dreads: 'I think about the literary world like I think about Tibet. It's quite interesting. It's a long way away from me, and it's sure as hell that they're never going to make me Dalai Lama.'

A strange phenomenon with these larger parties, unlike the smaller gatherings over which one has more control, is the number of people you end up with. Over the years, with the help of the dinner party book in which even publication parties are meticulously recorded, we have become adept at predicting the results. You wouldn't think that by sending out 181 invitations you would end up with eighty-nine guests, or that from a total of 112 you would receive sixty-eight acceptances. The strange thing is that the percentage of those attending rarely varies. In the absence of a train strike (the only one in the year which decimated one publication party) or an unseasonable fall of snow (which luckily came the day *after* one of our parties), 137 invitations will yield seventy-one guests, and 170 will bring forth ninety-nine. Unlike the dinner parties entries, which fit neatly on the page, these gatherings take up a great amount of space in the dinner party book and, the first one being full, I am now on volume two. The format for these occasions of course necessitates different forms of entry. One hundred and fourteen putative guests (of which seventy-three will turn up) cannot be written in the book round the picture of a dining table the capacity of which is twelve. Disregarding the drawing, intended for dinner parties, lists of their names are entered on the page under headings: 'invited', 'attended', 'unable', 'no show' and 'too rude to reply'. The post-mortem entries for these much anticipated bashes vary from the price per head (escalating yearly) to 'sandwiches too thick', 'more elderflower cordial needed' (people worried about driving) and 'asparagus (served griddled with dipping sauce) gritty'!

While many of these events, which span almost sixty years, were declared 'incredibly hard work', 'tiring' and 'exhausting – need help in the kitchen', the majority were recorded as 'perfect number', 'v. v. successful' and 'fantastic menu'. All in all, other than the times when it 'rained' on a garden party and 'B let us down' (I'm not sure now who he/she was nor why), the dinner party book is an invaluable document and – what could be more important – furnishes the history of a lifetime in friendship (not to mention food).

15

Paris Summer

The rule is, jam tomorrow and jam yesterday but never jam today.

LEWIS CARROLL

'Strike action left the entire tube network virtually paralysed today, causing travel chaos across the capital ...' Pickets manned key tube stations to deter would-be strike breakers as the RMT union called a 'twenty-four-hour action over pay and conditions'. Sympathetic as I felt towards the station staff who had downed tools in their battle to get a thirty-five-hour, four-day week and a minimum wage of £22,000 a year (rejected by Ken Livingstone, Mayor of London), I didn't see why, of all days to paralyse the tube network they had to choose 30 June 2004, the day of the publication party for *Paris Summer*. As a direct result of their action, according to the faithful dinner party book, although 157 people had been invited to the launch, only fifty – who lived nearby and had no qualms about getting home – turned up.

This setback, marred further by the rain which at six-thirty p.m. decided to fall on our terrace, was perhaps a reflection of the chequered history of the novel – about thwarted passion and the search for fulfilment and one of my favourites – which had at very long last made it into print. While I cannot regard *Paris Summer*'s emergence into the light of day as a defeat, the background to my twentieth novel was perhaps an object lesson, which every author learns early on in her career, that the writer, like the expectant mother, is always 'waiting' and should never give up.

Six years before the novel was published in hardback by John Hale, it was still doing the rounds of the studios as a film script, the form in which it had started life. Although Hollywood was always sending out messages that not enough good parts were written for 'older' actresses, directors Karel Reisz and John Schlesinger, and actors Meryl Streep and Paul Newman, were short-sighted enough to 'pass' on the script which had a forty-year-old woman as its protagonist and which was sent to them by my film agent, Linda Seifert. A plan by an independent BBC producer, Peter Kendal, to make the movie for the UK – with shooting to start in the spring – met a similar fate. Still undeterred, I put the *Paris Summer* script, together with several other irons I had in the fire, on a back burner and returned to the drawing board.

Most writers, at least those who have been in the business for any length of time, have several projects on the go at once. By no means all of them will come to fruition. We are always waiting. Upon the decisions of editors, the decrees of publishers, the whim of artistic directors. At the present time, and even at my age and so late in my career, I have four items in my 'expectations' file: an interest from a publisher to bring out those of my titles that have not already been produced in this format in large print ('we are snowed under at the moment, can you give us a couple of months?'); an offer to stage *An Eligible Man* in Turkey (of all places) as well as a putative tour of the same play planned by Ian Dickens, the biggest tour producer in the UK, to take place in the new year ('working on getting a cast together') and a possible English reprint by Hodder Children's Books of the popular *Aristide* and *Aristide in Paris* first published in the UK in 1966 and reissued in the French translation last year by Gallimard-Jeunesse in Paris ('unable to make a decision until after the Bologna Children's Book Fair'). Whether any or all of these projects will materialise is uncertain but it is the expectations that keep every writer going. We always have to be looking forward to something, and since we do not really 'live life to the full' as postulated by Henry James – we do not climb mountains, perform ground-breaking surgery or pilot the odd aircraft – but stare at the computer screen all day, having nothing on the cards, nothing to look forward to, would make for a very dull life indeed. This anticipation, this expectation, of what *might* happen, is what makes us look eagerly at our emails a hundred times a day, hoping that among them there will be a positive response from a publisher, some exciting news from theatre management or movie mogul – anything other than suggestions as to how to improve our sex lives, exhortations from chainstores begging us to buy their cut-price goods, or offers of free postage on our favourite kitchen gadgets.

While *Paris Summer*, the novel, started life as a film script, most film scripts are adaptations from novels and evolve the other way round. One of the reasons for this is that producers feel safer if they can capitalise on an established brand, be it a well-known author or a title. The Hollywood studios are always more interested in a property that has proved successful in another medium: Margaret Mitchell's *Gone with the Wind*, Graham Greene's *The Third Man*, Dashiell

Hammett's *The Maltese Falcon*, Pierre Boulle's *The Bridge on the River Kwai* ...

With very few, if any, exceptions, it is always a very long time – during which options, producers, scriptwriters and even authors will have come and gone – before the film versions of novels see the light of day. One such case is *Revolutionary Road*, the movie which in 2009 received nine Bafta nominations and procured both Golden Globe and Bafta awards for Kate Winslett as best actress. *Revolutionary Road*, adapted from Richard Yates's largely unheard of first novel (published almost half a century previously), finally hit the big screen seventeen years after the luckless author died, alone and in poverty, in Birmingham, Alabama, in 1992. While in his lifetime this hard-drinking World War Two veteran couldn't afford to go to college, worked as a freelance copywriter for Remington Rand, taught writing at Columbia and the University of Iowa, wrote occasional speeches for senator Robert F. Kennedy, collected countless rejection slips and attracted withering reviews, on the back of the successful movie his books have only now been reissued and are selling well.

Sam Mendes was not the first director to attempt to bring Yates's novel – in which, as in my own novel *Paris Summer*, 'Paris' is a metaphor for escape, where you can roll back the years, a place where you can successfully recapture your lost youth – to the screen. While none of Yates's seven novels and three collections of short stories ever sold more than 1,200 copies in his lifetime and the author was the recipient of mixed reviews and hundreds of rejection slips, and lived his life in poor health, with multiple nervous breakdowns (he suffered from bipolar disorder), he knew that eventually he would transcend the times and that ultimately his work would outlive him. This, of course, is the goal of every writer and not very many of the hundreds and thousands – if not millions – of us bashing away at our keyboards on a daily basis achieve it. Success turns on the most elusive spin of the dice.

If Kate Winslett had not taken a fancy to the idea and sold it to her then husband, director Sam Mendes, a film version of Yates's *Revolutionary Road* would still be languishing. Although many producers, including Scott Rudin – thirty years after, as a young casting director, he had discovered the novel – had failed to get the movie made, it was not for want of trying. Director John Frankenheimer and producer Al Ruddy acquired the rights for $15,500 and sold them on to actor Patrick O'Neal, who generated a screenplay. Yates did not approve of it and tried to buy back the rights but O'Neal insisted on keeping them. It was only after his death that the BBC sent Winslett *their* version of the script, this time by American novelist and screenwriter Justin Haythe. Early on in this chain of events, Scott Rudin tried to claw back the movie rights from Al Ruddy but he didn't have the money. He had, however, worked with Sam Mendes in London and New York (*Blue Room*) and had produced *Iris,* in which Kate Winslett played the late Iris Murdoch. When this time Kate Winslett approached him with *Revolutionary Road* he thought that her husband, Sam Mendes, could bring out some of the same qualities he had in Brian Friel's play *Translations* – in which the two leads share a love scene without speaking the same language – and in the fullness of time, and *forty-eight* years after the novel was written, the movie finally got made.

There are countless other examples of screenplays from novels that are passed from studio to studio and producer to producer and either take aeons to get made or fall by the wayside. While stories are filtered, infinitesimally slowly, through screenwriters, directors, cinematographers, studio chiefs and a variety of other hands, only an average of thirty novels a year make it to the big screen.

Some of the finest novels do not make it at all. Gabriel García Márquez's *One Hundred Years of Solitude*, an astounding piece of fiction, both passionate and amusing, has resisted the camera partly perhaps because it has no central character, and partly because it is surreal; while a few attempts have been made (one starring Catherine Deneuve and John Malkovich) to bring Marcel Proust's *Remembrance of Things Past*, with its scents, sounds and certain objects pushing associated memories to the fore, none has proved successful; although Franz Kafka's *The Trial* has been done, *Metamorphosis*, in which the protagonist, Gregor Samsa, awakes to find himself a giant insect, has proved more difficult and although many attempts have been made to film Miguel de Cervantes's *Don Quixote* – Orson Welles spent much of his life trying to make the film but failed to complete it – a satisfactory version has never been seen on the screen. Classics such as Charles Dickens's *A Christmas Carol*, E. M. Forster's *Passage to India*, Evelyn Waugh's *Brideshead Revisited*, Boris Pasternak's epic *Dr Zhivago* and Alexandre Dumas's *The Count of Monte Cristo* have fared better, as have faithful modern adaptations such as Dan Brown's *The Da Vinci Code*, Peter Benchley's *Jaws*, Stephen King's *The Shawshank Redemption* and J. R. R. Tolkien's *Lord of the Rings*. *Slumdog Millionaire* (adapted by screenwriter Simon Beaufoy from the 2005 novel *Q & A* by Indian author and diplomat Vikas Swarup), in which an impoverished Mumbai teenager becomes a contestant on the Indian version of *Who Wants to Be a Millionaire?* and is arrested for cheating, is a runaway success, as is any novel from the pen of the prolific Ian Fleming from *Casino Royale*, through *Diamonds Are Forever*, *From Russia with Love*, *Goldfinger*, *Live and Let Die*, *Man with the Golden Gun*, *The Spy Who Loved Me* and *You Only Live Twice* – all of which, together with many others, have been sure-fire winners. Film-from-novel adaptation is a rocky road and it is not always the finest fiction writers who ride it.

Despite my novel-from-film script, *Paris Summer*, having been more or less politely rejected by eleven major publishing houses – rejections they blamed variously on the times (hard), the lists (full), and the subject matter (already done better by someone else) – which many less stoical authors would have regarded as not only a defeat but a rout, Robert Hale who eventually published it, Adrian George who produced the jacket, and Claire Bowles who was in charge of publicity, made a good enough fist of it. Although the two film options taken out on the novel eventually came to nought and the promised paperback failed to materialise, the long-running project had at long last come to fruition and despite the train strike that threatened to scupper the celebrations at the last moment, had finally not only made it into print but was subsequently published in a 'large print' edition by Thorpe (with a beautiful picture of the Eiffel Tower on the jacket), and the audio rights bought by Isis, the largest of 'talking-book' producers.

This again had its downturns. When the contract was signed, I enquired if my friend, the well-known American actress Gayle Hunnicutt (then married to Simon Jenkins, one-time editor of *The Times* and now Sir Simon), would be allowed to read *Paris Summer* for audio. Isis, of course, were delighted to be able to use so well-known a name (a guarantee of sales) and, despite her reservations, Gayle agreed to undertake the task. And task it was. Producing a novel on tape required that the reader leave her home and spend three weeks in a studio in the Midlands where the text was recorded on a daily basis. The actor's reservation was that she was not too keen on associating herself with a heroine who commits adultery, a subject upon which she had strong puritanical views. Pointing out that in the end the protagonist stays with her husband, I managed to twist her arm. She agreed to do the job and was about to sign the contract with Isis, when once again, through no fault of my own, my plans for *Paris Summer* were foiled. Gayle's mother was taken ill and she had to go to Texas! In the end, the book was read by an English actor whose pseudo-Bostonian accent failed to bring the book to life.

Rain and the train strike notwithstanding, the launch of *Paris Summer* was a great success. Although there is no formula, I have learned over the years that the secret of a good publication party, like the formula for a good cocktail, is to mix it well. In addition to friends (his and hers) and family (his, hers and ours) of all ages, I always invite anyone who cares to come from the publishing house – from the newest recruit to the publicity department to the CEO – and others who I think will add spice to the occasion. The bash for *Paris Summer* included authors Moris Farhi (now OBE for services to literature), Francis King CBE, and best-selling crime writer Peter James, biographers Ronald Hayman (Harold Pinter, Arthur Miller, Fassbinder, Sartre, Thomas Mann and Jung) and Brenda Maddox (Rosalind Franklin, W. B. Yeats, Nora Joyce, Ernest Jones and Freud), the late stage and television actor William Franklyn, artist

Adrian George, publisher Peter Owen, Professor of Oncology Jonathan Waxman, Professor of Surgery Gerald Westbury, Professor of Biology, anatomist and media guru Lewis Wolpert, Professor of Endocrinology Dame Julia Polak, Professor of Haematology Daniel Catovsky and Ilsa Yardley, who had been my literary agent until her retirement. Psychiatrists, film distributors, PEN officials, booksellers and grandchildren added to the brew and, according to the entry in my dinner party book, everyone behaved themselves, the party was 'v. successful' and, despite the fact that due to the exceptional circumstances there were twenty-five 'no shows' and only fifty people actually managed to turn up, 'no food was left!'

16

The Human Condition

Always too eager for the future, we pick up bad habits of expectancy.

PHILIP LARKIN

I was a sickly child – one of my earliest memories was of having my tonsils removed at home on the kitchen table – who in addition to all the contemporary maladies such as measles, mumps, chicken-pox and whooping-cough developed tubercular glands in the neck, which necessitated further surgery. Adolescence and motherhood brought other interventions including the surgical removal of all four impacted wisdom teeth, two cystoscopies, two operations for an infected ear (before the advent of antibiotics), a laparotomy for an ongoing abdominal pain, which turned out to be due to adhesions from the earlier appendicectomy, excision of a breast lump (fibroadenoma) – mercifully benign – leading to a haematoma, which required draining, a hysterectomy following a series of uterine infections after the birth of my fourth daughter, and sundry other procedures too trivial to mention.

An acute intestinal obstruction, treated conservatively but necessitating three weeks as an in-patient in the Middlesex

Hospital (now defunct) being fed through a nasal-gastro tube, was followed by the relentless march of osteoarthritis affecting the joints, and a variety of eye diseases with quaintly pompous appellations such as 'Theodore's superior limbic kerato conjunctivitis', 'chronic meibomium gland disease', 'redundant bulbar conjunctiva' and pseudoexfoliation, most of which came under the less technical umbrella of 'sore and inflamed eyes' treated permanently and several times a day with steroidal and non-steroidal drops. These inconveniences, combined with the Ramsay Hunt syndrome, which struck some sixteen years ago (see *The Writing Game*) and left me with a facial palsy, a permanently metallic taste in the mouth and inability to close one eye properly, have miraculously never stopped me from working, which once the floodgates are fully open 'banishes the disagreeables'. It is gratifying to know that among writers and artists, as far as physical disease is concerned, I am not alone. Creative ability has long been linked with the pain, loss and the desperation associated with mental illness (see *The Writing Game*) as suffered by a long line of artists, musicians and writers, including, among many others, Vincent Van Gogh, Robert Schumann, Sylvia Plath and Virginia Woolf.

Many writers – as becomes manifest when a few of them get together – are also plagued by physical complaints, despite which – or perhaps because of which – they manage to produce considerable bodies of work. Leo Tolstoy suffered variously from rheumatism, enteritis, toothaches, fainting spells, malaria, phlebitis, typhoid fever and several small strokes, while Lewis Carroll had to contend with ague, cystitis, lumbago, boils, eczema, synovitis, rheumatism, neuralgia, insomnia and toothaches, a troublesome stammer and partial deafness. Samuel Beckett's teeth were bad, his neck hurt, he had pleurisy and his feet gave him hell. John Betjeman had Parkinson's disease, Christy Brown cerebral palsy, Emily Dickinson and Jonathan Swift Meunières disease, John Updike psoriasis, Agatha Christie, Charles Dickens, Michelangelo, Leonardo da Vinci, Edgar Allan Poe and Aristotle epilepsy, Stephen Hawking Amyotrophic Lateral Sclerosis (ALS), and Homer, James Thurber, Galileo Galilei and Jorge Luis Borges were either totally blind or visually challenged.

Peripheral neuropathy, diagnosed in 2006 when I was seventy-seven, was a new turn-up for the books and thought to be partly due to the chemotherapy I had previously undergone for the lymphoma. When I began to find it more and more difficult and painful to walk, when, even with bare feet, I felt as if I still had tight socks on and the touch of the bedclothes turned said feet into an oxymoron of 'burning ice', I realised that a new inconvenience was on the agenda. Peripheral neuropathy describes damage to the peripheral nervous system, the vast communications network that transmits information from the brain and autonomic nervous system to every other part of the body. Peripheral nerves also send sensory information back to the spinal cord, such as a message that the feet are cold or a finger is burned. Damage to the peripheral nervous system interferes with these vital connections. Like the static on a telephone system, peripheral neuropathy distorts, and sometimes interrupts, messages between the brain and the rest of the body. Because every peripheral nerve has a highly specialised function in a specific part of the body, a wide array of symptoms can occur when nerves are damaged. These include: temporary numbness, tingling and pricking sensations (paresthesia), sensitivity to touch or muscle weakness. Other symptoms include burning pain, especially at night (which accounted for the sensations in my feet), muscle wasting, paralysis and organ or gland dysfunction. In more extreme cases breathing is affected and organ failure might occur.

More hospital visits, fortunately again to Barts, where my patient credentials were already established, included electromyography (EMG), a test which entails needle electrodes being inserted through the skin into the muscles of the feet and legs. The electrical activity detected by these electrodes is displayed on an oscilloscope and it can also be heard through a speaker. The presence, size and shape of the wave form – the 'action potential' – provides information about the ability of the muscle to respond when the nerves are stimulated. A nerve conduction velocity test confirmed what the consultant neurologist, to whom I was referred, had suspected. A diagnosis was made and peripheral neuropathy officially added to my growing catalogue of infirmities which, like the insidious onset of age with its increasing frailty and loss of elasticity in the skin (wrinkles), it is hard to get one's mind around.

Like most things in life, this last, annoying and often extremely painful condition had its upside. I had always raised a sceptical eyebrow at lissom ladies who, while sporting the highest of heels and moving with awesome speed, displayed the Blue European Parking badges (which had replaced the Orange Disabled Persons Badge) on the windscreens of their 4 × 4s. When, as my mobility became increasingly impaired and I was unable both to walk to the shops and shop – it was one or the other – it was suggested by my neurologist, who wrote a letter supporting my claim, that I should apply for one such badge which, having previously considered that only those in wheelchairs merited the privilege, I did with some reservation. Having completed the application form together with proof of residence, two photographs signed on the back and the appropriate documentary evidence, and submitted them to the Permit Administration Department of Camden Council, my claim was assessed by an independent doctor who asked searching questions such as how far I was able to walk and how much pain I was in, to establish the extent of mobility impairment. Having examined my feet and legs, he made copious notes and filled in copious forms and, giving nothing away at the time, said that in due course I would be hearing from the Council who, under the rules of the scheme, would make the ultimate decision to grant, or refuse, a Blue Badge. There was no right of appeal.

In the fullness of time I received a letter from Transport for London informing me that my application for a Blue Badge had been successful and that my registration entitled me to a hundred per cent discount when using my 'long-term vehicle' – aka my car – from the congestion charge. This benefit meant that I could drive into town on any day that I wished and as many times as I wished without having to pay for the privilege, and that I was eligible for free parking on designated disabled bays. There were other benefits to go with the Blue Badge (renewed every three years by means of new photographs, an up-to-date assessment form signed by the Occupational Therapist for the London Borough of Camden, and fresh proof of residence) which must be clearly displayed on the near-side dashboard or fascia panel of the car together with the parking disc or 'clock'. While Camden Council, with its high taxation rates, could be faulted on its disinclination to collect the garbage sufficiently frequently and to keep its streets clean from the detritus left by the indigent winos, it did, extraordinarily, allow its Blue Badge holders to park their cars for considerable periods of time free on parking meters, as well as on residents' bays and either single or – incredibly – double yellow lines. This meant that those of us permitted to do so could park directly outside our local Marks & Spencer or Ryness, the electrical store, when we needed to replace a recalcitrant light bulb or had laddered our tights. There were other privileges, of all of which I felt guilty of availing myself and fraudulent when I did so: half-price theatre and concert tickets (obtained by registering with the access schemes of the Royal National Theatre or the Albert Hall), together with free car parking at the former. Other theatres also had their discount schemes.

While I would far rather have turned back the clock and regained my previous agility – how much we take for granted – and freedom from pain, as far as my writing was concerned I could not complain. Lord Byron, with his club foot, did not allow his disability to get in the way of his poetry, poor blind Milton turned out exquisite verse and Elizabeth Barrett Browning was never short of a word or two although confined for much of her life – for reasons that still remain a mystery – to her chaise longue. Society in general has frequently underestimated the capabilities of people with chronic illnesses and disregarded the fact that physical disability, unlike some mental disorders, does not diminish creativity, the action of making, forming, producing or bringing into existence that which did not exist before.

This creativity was something that those unable to write, paint or compose were at a loss to understand. We hardly understood it ourselves and when interviewed for magazines or newspapers or had our brains picked by dinner-table companions anxious to know how it was done, frequently had to make up the answers:

INQUISITOR: What made you become a writer?
WRITER: [*How on earth do I know?*] Maybe I wanted to write a book I would enjoy reading or a play I'd like to see. From the moment you sit down at your desk you can visualise your novel already bound, your play produced. Writing is convenient. It needs no training and very few tools. You're too busy writing to wonder what demons are driving you.
INQUISITOR: Do you write every day or only when you get the inspiration?
WRITER: Every day. [*This is a lie. See next chapter.*] William Faulkner said: 'I don't know anything about inspiration because I don't know what inspiration is – I've heard about it but I never saw it.' The act of writing inspires me. It's a nice feeling. If you're not at your computer you're writing in your head. It's all there. There's no need to think about it. Writing *is* thinking. It's an arrangement of words. Sixty-five to a hundred thousand of them and it's hard work getting them down on paper. At first you think that it's not even within the realm of possibility … It's a full-time job.
INQUISITOR: Where do you get your ideas?
WRITER: [*Stupid question, I'll try.*] In the beginning there's something very nebulous, a state of alert, a wariness, a curiosity. Ideas materialise. They come into your head. Usually several at a time: very vague at first, could be a character, the ghost of a plot … The idea that refuses to go away is the one that gets worked on. Great ideas and scientific discoveries frequently occur in different parts of the world

at the same time, and there is often a doubling up in the film world where two or more films cover similar material almost concurrently (*Capote*, and *Infamous*, both of them biopics about Truman Capote), but where one took nearly 30 million dollars the other only 2.6 million. It's the same with writers. They make use of the *zeitgeist*, pick up ideas that are already in the air.

INQUISITOR: Do you do much research?

WRITER: [*That old chestnut!*] The whole of life is a writer's compost heap. No matter what we are doing – reading, travelling, talking to friends and acquaintances, listening to other people's conversations in the pharmacy or post office, on the train or in the bus – we are collecting data and squirrelling it away. Most writing is done away from your desk. While you're walking in the park, or cooking, or washing your hair or chatting to someone you're not all that interested in. It's a concentrated form of thinking. You don't really know what you think until you try to write about it. According to Alan Plater: 'It's about listening. And writing it down. If you stop listening and you lose that curiosity about the way people speak and the way people behave, then you stop being a proper writer.' A writer pays close attention to the world. You beg, borrow or steal from anybody and everybody to get the work done. You need time to think. To work things out. Once the floodgates are open everything you experience exists only in relation to your writing. You make use of every little thing. For the duration of the work in progress you lead a kind of permanent double life. It's very exhausting.

INQUISITOR: How does it feel to write a novel?

WRITER: Edith Wharton summed it up: 'The beginning: A ride through a spring wood. The middle: The Gobi desert. The end: A night with a lover.'

INQUISITOR: How long does it take you?

WRITER: [*How long is a piece of string?*] Six months, twelve months, two years. It depends what else you're doing, what coincidental alarums and excursions there are. It's very difficult. Sometimes I write my shopping lists, check my bank statements, find every pretext not to work. That doesn't happen very often. Once I've started I work quite fast. When I finish a book I don't really believe that I've written it. It was written by my arms, my brain … some independent organism with a mind of its own.

INQUISITOR: How do you feel when you're not working?

WRITER: [*Like now!*] That I'm wasting my time, my life.

INQUISITOR: Are there any books you would like to have written?

WRITER: [*Of course.*] I write what I can. I do my best.

INQUISITOR: What other interests do you have?

WRITER: *[Are there other interests?]* Writing consumes all your time, all your energy. Other people, people with different minds, have all sorts of other interests, other activities going on.

INQUISITOR: Are you still writing as much as you did?

WRITER: ['*Are you still writing*'!] When you are young you have boundless energy. You run the house and care for your children and see your friends and family and go to evening classes and the theatre and write … I don't know how I did it. I couldn't do it all now. You get slower when you get older. You have to pace yourself. Your memory gets worse. Writing a novel is like holding the plans of a cathedral in your head. It's not so easy any more.

INQUISITOR: How many hours a day do you write?

WRITER: [*I don't count them.*] I start about six-thirty in the morning and go on until about twelve-thirty or before that if

I am empty, if I run dry. Then I do other things, go through the motions, visitors, household … the mundane things. It's easier for men. Nothing means very much. I get through the day the best I can and wait for the next morning when the pumps are primed. It's the waiting that's hard.

INQUISITOR: What about social life?

WRITER: [*What about it?*] I don't have much. It's draining. I don't really need it. I find it difficult to work the next day. By and large it's a waste of time. I lead rather a solitary life. It's hard on my husband. I am irritable in the mornings when I'm raring to write. I find it hard to concentrate, to give my full attention to other things. '*Longtemps je me suis couché de bonne heure.*' Like Proust I like to go to bed early, read or go to a film.

INQUISITOR: Do you get fan mail from readers?

WRITER: [*Fortunately/Unfortunately.*] Frequently. It's very gratifying. They think they have a right to you, particularly if you have a new book out. As if they own you.

INQUISITOR: Do you reply to them?

WRITER: [*I feel bound to.*] I keep in touch. Widows from Solihull, retired teachers. Often handwritten, blue ink on blue paper. Sometimes they want a photograph. To use as a bookmark. And demand that you keep writing not only 'for' them but 'to' them. They tell you their life – 'more an existence really' – stories, details of hospital visits, medical histories … Make you feel guilty. It's not difficult. Writers spend their lives feeling guilty. For not working (not having a 'proper' job), for being able to do something others would give their right arms for, for not providing satisfactory answers to inquisitors who hope to get the key to creativity, to find out – from the last person to ask and who has not the slightest idea – how it is done.

17

All Mod. Con.

No day is commonplace if we had only eyes to see its splendour.

RALPH WALDO EMERSON

We have come a long way since Virginia Woolf remarked, 'If there was chicken, she took the leg; if there was a draught, she sat in it' and Simone de Beauvoir wrote, '... If woman is earthly, commonplace, basely utilitarian, it is because she is compelled to devote her existence to cooking and washing diapers – no way to acquire a true sense of grandeur!'

Or have we? It was all very well for Georges Simenon to boast '... when I am doing a novel now I don't see anybody, I don't speak to anybody, I don't make a phone call – I live just like a monk' but the reason why most women (and probably most men) writers find it difficult to give a true answer to the Inquisitor as to how long it takes to write a book is because of the interruptions to her work schedule. Given the difficulties and problems of the modern world, never mind the writing (or the demands of a legal practice, the hassle of running a hospital department or the workload of a financial institution) you could easily spend your life 'just living'. No matter how much of a 'new man' – a highly suspicious epithet – your husband or partner (assuming you have one), no matter how hard you determine to prioritise your writing (first things first), there are always extraneous tasks to be carried out – even Shakespeare's sister was too busy 'mending stockings or tending to the stew' to write her poetry – and there is always something that must be done, your 'internal desk' is never completely clear.

If there are meals to be planned (we can't always live on takeaways), lists have to be made, shopping has to be done (even if you use a delivery service and even if your partner does it) and ultimately goods put away and packaging (should you succeed in removing it) disposed of according to its recyclability. Notebooks, or pages of the desk diary on which you ostensibly keep details of your work or lunches and meetings with agents and publishers are littered with jottings and hieroglyphs, *aides mémoires* such as 'pots, mush, toms', 'chick 4 Sunday', 'b'day card', 'avos', '2-hole punch', 'smkd haddock', 'watch mend', '9V batts', 'COPY PAPER (urgent)', '?plumber', 'gift-wrap' and 'road fund licence!!!'.

Of course the internet – if your temperamental server doesn't get the hump and is not too busy – has made life easier. In a manner of speaking: if you can remember your IDs and passwords (case sensitive) and answers to security questions lost in the mists of time and your mother's maiden name and your credit card number and start date and expiry date and three-digit security code and the web page doesn't expire and you are not advised by the computer in the thick of the action that 'one of your disks needs to be checked' or updates run 'please restart your machine' and you don't forget to click 'confirm'. The advent of the computer was supposed to herald the paperless office but printouts of vital emails – agreements to publish or not to publish, to stage or not to stage – which must be filed for future reference insist on spewing out not only the relevant data but spare pages blank except for one line of gobbledegook which reads something like *http:/by115.mail.live.com/mail/InboxLight.aspx?n=585641879* and you wonder how many rainforests have been denuded to provide you with this indecipherable and superfluous information. The emails themselves, those to do with your work – friends send me jokes or space-hogging jpegs or round-robins at their peril – are buried amidst missives from airlines offering reduced fares and increased miles/points to exotic locations you have no intention of visiting, and discounted tickets at theatres for musicals you have no wish to see, and new arrivals at mailorder stores whose websites you once unwisely visited, and how to reduce your energy bills and how much you can save at Amazon.co.uk and bargain shirts (mid-season sale now on) and tempting offers from art galleries and museums.

The telephone, invented simply to send and receive sound – most commonly speech – between two people, by means of transmitting electric signals over some kind of network is no better. Innocenzo Manzetti, Antonio Meucci, Johann Philipp Reis, Elisha Gray, Alexander Graham Bell and Thomas Edison, all credited with the pioneer work on the device intended to save time and make life simpler, must be turning in their graves. A quick call to secure a service visit for a malfunctioning piece of domestic equipment or electrical fault or indeed to the telephone company itself, necessitates being 'put on hold' (we know you are waiting, your call is important to us) and listening to options that rarely address your particular problem and lead to further exponential choices, which seldom result in the dialogue with the fellow human being you are seeking and, should they so do, the unfamiliar cadences of accents from Aberdeen or Agra defeat the original purpose of facilitating communication between two human beings which the telephone pioneers had in mind. Often you could weep. At the daily frustrations. At the chronic waste of time spent on obtaining the simplest of results which were achieved in moments when your destination was reached by manually – inserting your fingers into the holes – dialling telephone exchanges consisting of three simple letters, WEL (Welbeck) or MAY (Mayfair) followed by four numbers and zero for the operator who didn't order you to listen to a menu before pressing a dozen buttons or threaten that your call might be recorded and used for 'training purposes' (training purposes?) and who would politely connect you if you wanted to make a 'trunk' (i.e. long distance) call. We know about the population explosion and the fact that there are too many people on our tiny island but you would think that with the advent of technology and our ability to send human beings into space we would have managed to save rather than waste time on maintaining our habitats and getting our lives sorted.

Allowing too much time to pass when engaged tête-à-tête with the computer is often counterproductive. Putting the washing into the machine, emptying the dishwasher or carrying out other essential household chores is therapeutic and provides a welcome and necessary physical break from the inertia and inadvisability of staring for any longer than a few hours at a time at the screen. These self-imposed tasks at selected intervals provide welcome breaks for snacks (a thousand words merit one chocolate biscuit) and cups of coffee, and in no way impinge on the creative flow. It is the countless other interruptions that impede the work in progress and which are *sui generis* frustrating. Bills must be paid, albeit online where financial transactions – if you can recall the date you last logged in to your bank account – are also carried out.

A reluctant shopper, my forays into the consumer world are now, and have been for many years, carried out without leaving my desk as groceries, cosmetics, clothes, books, stationery, household appliances and kitchen gadgets are purchased at the click of a mouse. This, of course, brings its own downside and precious time is wasted in the effort involved in packing up things to be returned when they don't do what it says on the tin or live up to expectations or you failed to notice that the sizes quoted were *American,* and in locating the sticky tape and struggling to get a grip on the irretrievably gummed-up end and realising as you finally leave the house to join the post-office queue (our local post office is threatened with closure and a letter of protest must be written) that you've failed to put the slip with your name and address and reason for sending the items back inside the parcel. These are the minor irritations, the lesser interruptions in a life in which any time spent 'not writing' is bitterly resented.

Even when you think you've got a 'clean' day – one in which you can devote yourself to your work – if not a 'clean' week, the sun is shining, which reminds you to put away your winter wardrobe, which must be washed or dry-cleaned (to deter the moths) and replacing it with your summer one (vice versa in the autumn), a letter from the DVLA will advise you that your driving licence needs renewing, your vacuum cleaner will have run out of bags, your pillbox out of pills, your stapler out of staples, your fax machine out of film and your printer needs a new cartridge; your passport is on its last legs (two new photographs, please, look straight at the camera and remove your glasses) and an impossible year has gone by and your tax returns are due; someone will have inconsiderately decided to fall ill or have an operation and go into hospital, predicating books or flowers and time-consuming visits (presuming you can find somewhere to park) which you try hard, in the interests of your work, which has just grown wings and assumed a life of its own, not to resent; a death – more frequent at one's time of life – be it friends or family, cannot be taken so lightly and means a greater commitment in terms of funerals to attend and mourners to comfort and a more prolonged downing of tools, not to mention the concomitant grief that must be worked through; holiday destinations have to be explored, again on the internet (and often in the midst of a chapter), flights, if they are not to cost an arm and a leg, booked well in advance, and an extra week set aside for packing a suitcase – which, like writing a novel, entails several drafts – and cancelling the newspapers and sorting out the contents of the fridge, and another week on your return for dealing with the laundry and putting away the holiday gear and doing battle with the accumulated emails and letters. And just when you think you have turned the corner and from now on it will be plain sailing you will lose a filling or sit on your specs or catch a cold or (horrors!) the flu and you have no choice but to down tools for a few hours, a few days or a week.

Sometimes the disturbers of your hard-fought-for peace wear a human face. No sooner have you eagerly typed Chapter One, or Two, or Three at the top of your screen when the telephone, which you can't resist answering, rings and an excited voice informs you that Sally from the States or April from Australia are – 'you're not going to believe this' – not only in town but staying for what is to be a whistle-stop tour not a million miles from where you live. While you decide whether a quick lunch, a slow (catch-up) dinner or a play or a movie they are dying to see or are raring to take you to, will be the least disruptive of your schedule, they will reassure you that they guess you are probably in the midst of some *grande oeuvre* and would not be so inconsiderate as to take up much of your precious time. But as they speak your heart has already sunk and your muse has left by the nearest window, and you are wondering why you haven't bothered to wash your hair for days and whether it would be less trouble to drag round a museum or gallery you are not in the mood for or, remembering their unstinting culinary efforts when you found yourself in Cairns or Orange County, conjure up a time-consuming dinner while trying to remember who it was who said: 'I will give you my love but not my time.'

These are not the only disturbances to what, when your children have long ago grown up and left home, should be a fertile time for writing. Life, in fact, seemed more simple, more easy to get a grip on and to cope with when they were young and there were seven (including the au pair) mouths to feed three times a day and fifty-six (yes fifty-six) white socks and thirty-five pairs of knickers not bunged higgledy-piggledy into the tumble dryer but hanging, pristine, like so many flags, on the weekly washing line.

At least, when we have liberated adequate gobbets of time and maintained the ancient monument in terms of visits to the doctor and the podiatrist (chiropodist) and beauty salon and increasingly frequent dental and ophthalmic care, we are free to write, and free to write what we want. Now and again, these frivolous demands upon one's time are put sharply into perspective.

One of the advantages of belonging to English PEN, a registered charity with a commitment to promote literature and human rights, is that through the Writers in Prison Committee, on which I no longer serve (having sent books to prisoners for many years) and the Rapid Action Network, which calls upon members to protest against the sentences and to call for the release of prisoners in accordance with Article 19 of the United Nations Universal Declaration of Human Rights, for which I do my bit, is that one is kept in touch with fellow writers whose voices have been repressed or silenced. In the past year alone, 133 of those writers and journalists who have dared to put their heads above the parapet in the face of perceived injustice, have been imprisoned, 190 are under judicial process, ninety-three have been attacked, eighty are under death threats, seven have disappeared and twenty-four have been killed. A Mexican journalist and his family have been threatened and there are fears for his safety, there are health concerns for jailed writers in China, a detained internet writer in Iran has died under suspicious circumstances and journalists in Columbia have been threatened and intimidated. The impressive case list of writers supported by PEN is worldwide and covers Africa and the Americas, Asia and the Pacific, Europe and Central Asia and the Middle East; Somalia and Senegal, Cuba and Haiti, Gambia and Gabon, Venezuela and Thailand, South Korea and Senegal, Kazakhstan and Turkey, Ethiopia and Chad.

As I write, the network has been alerted to the plight of three Burmese dissidents who are facing harsh sentences in Myanmar. A leading comedian and poet has been handed down an astonishing forty-five-year prison sentence and is believed to have been punished for his outspoken criticism of his government's slow response to Cyclone Nargis: it is feared that even more years could be added to his prison sentence; a fifteen-year sentence has similarly been given to a journalist who was arrested – and had his computer, mobile phone and personal documents confiscated – while visiting his sick mother in central Burma, on a charge of providing a private relief effort to deliver aid and support to victims of the cyclone; another poet, Saw Wei, and musician, Win Maw, were also sentenced in what the BBC described as 'a judicial crackdown across the spectrum of Burma's pro-democracy movement'.

The latest appeal to PEN members has been to write letters of support on behalf of honorary member Jorge Olivera Castillo, a Cuban poet who was one of the thirty-five journalists, writers and librarians arrested during the 2003 'Black Spring' crackdown on alleged dissidents who, after one-day hearings held behind closed doors with the accused denied time to put together cogent defences, received prison sentences ranging from fourteen to twenty-seven years. Seven years later, twenty-two of them are still in prison. After twenty months and eighteen days in prison (often in solitary confinement) Jorge Olivera was released on health grounds. He had lost thirteen kilos and was suffering from high blood pressure and serious infections. Following PEN's nomination last year, Olivera has been offered a fellowship within the Department of Literature and Comparative Literature at Harvard and members are petitioning the President of Cuba, the Interior Minister, the Minister of Foreign Affairs and the Minister of Culture requesting that he be given permission to leave the island temporarily in order to take up the post. The appeal is purely literary and scholarly (we do not identify ourselves as PEN members) and no political statements or statements regarding his imprisonment are made.

The Writers in Prison Committee lobbies for the release of such prisoners and encourages others to do so. The testimonies of hundreds of writers it has represented over the past forty years are witness to the fact that their efforts have been instrumental in keeping the despair and loneliness of those who have been incarcerated and often held in solitary confinement at bay. They offer solidarity with international colleagues not only by making them honorary members of a local PEN centre but by sending cards, letters and books, which provide hope for the future.

Inconvenient and time-consuming as it may be, writing letters of protest to the movers and shakers in the appropriate countries, to their diplomatic representative in the UK and to the national newspapers, is, in the face of the harsh sentences handed down to fellow writers, a small enough price for those of us lucky enough to be living and working in the free world to pay.

18

Start Right

Ah, yes, I remember it well ...

MAURICE CHEVALIER

'*Plus ça change plus c'est la même chose*.' Not true. One of the advantages of living for such a very long time is that you can see the world in perspective, flag the changes, infinitesimal to some, which have taken place over your lifetime. Despite the collapse of the Soviet Union, the smashing of the Berlin Wall, the end of apartheid, the installation of the first black President of the USA, our almost nonchalant conquest of space and the disappearance of the national anthem from cinemas, one of the minor but most fascinating metamorphoses I have witnessed since my youth is the advent, a leitmotif of our times, of the commercial 'sandwich'. Sixty-odd years ago, when I was a child, sandwich fillings were largely jam, raspberry or strawberry, sometimes, on party occasions, egg-and-cress or fish paste (Shipham's), and occasionally, as a rare treat when a rib of beef had been roasted on Sundays, dripping, the semi-solidified fat from the joint with its rough impression and indescribable savoury taste on the tongue. These sandwiches, of various thicknesses according to the skill of the cutter, were hewn from solid rectangular loaves – made from a basic white bread dough and baked in a pan known universally as 'tin' – with a serrated knife kept especially for the purpose. While my mother cut bread on to a designated board, my grandmother held the loaf against her not inconsiderable and well-corseted bosom and sliced perilously towards her chest. Surprising as it may seem in the light of the fact that there was no such thing as 'Health and Safety' regulations to deter her, she never had an accident, the slices were of uniform thickness and the knife, to my knowledge, never slipped.

As far as bread and butter was concerned, there were two schools of thought. Those in one camp buttered (or margarined) the bread *before* cutting it, and the other, *afterwards*, praying that there were no holes in the loaf. The sandwich, having been assembled and divided, generally into four squares (crusts *on* in the mythical interests of curly hair), was either put on a plate if it was to be eaten for tea at home or, for want of the cling film or tinfoil we take for granted today, wrapped in unyielding 'greaseproof' paper for consumption at school, on the ubiquitous picnic, or elsewhere. There was absolutely no question of either bread that had been pre-sliced in a factory by an impersonal machine at no risk to the bosom, or a ready-made sandwich with a corpus of fillings, that could be bought, individually wrapped and at considerable expense, from every other shop on the high street.

The sandwich was not the only new kid on the block since I started out eighty-odd years ago. If the proverbial 'man from Mars', my grandmother, or even my parents were to drop by today they would be amazed to discover that the 'macaroni cheese', which they created from scratch from milk, delivered daily to the doorstep in glass bottles by the milkman with his horse-drawn float (with its inevitable trail, which provided manure for the garden), from butter and cheese meticulously weighed out in chunks on cast-iron scales in the local Sainsbury's by ladies with hair restrained by muslin snoods, could be bought ready-made from the supermarket – a marvel in its own right – and heated in seconds in the eighth wonder of the world, the microwave oven. Whether, in a blind tasting, the contents of the brightly decorated box with its foil lining and terse instructions to 'remove cover, pierce film and place on a baking tray' would pass muster when compared with the home-made, home-cooked version, its sauce fashioned from a 'roux' of butter and flour, its cheese painstakingly grated, its macaroni shovelled loose from a giant sack into a brown-paper bag and carried home in a shopping basket, is questionable.

While twentieth-century phenomena such as aeroplanes and nuclear power, television and the internet have changed our lives out of all recognition, inventions of more humble origin that today we take for granted – the paper clip, the ballpoint pen, the credit card, the pocket calculator and the Pill – would also leave our forebears flummoxed.

We look back in amazement at the squalor and filth of the early nineteenth century with its unwashed bodies and sewage-filled gutters, at Dickens's blacking factory, his workhouse, his debtors' prison and the premature death of Little Nell for want of a few modern-day antibiotics, and forget the metamorphoses that have taken place in our own century and which define our times. While the Victorians gave us electric power and light, the telephone, the radio, photography, the motor car and the railway, which led to the spread of such labour-saving devices as washing machines, vacuum cleaners and food mixers that purportedly changed the lives of women for the better, our own century has also seen the rise of the aerosol, with its devastating effect on the ozone layer, the chainsaw, which has become the means for the destruction of the rainforests, disposable nappies and other products that clog the environment, the parking meter, which generates rage and indignation on our over-crowded city streets and takeaway meals of every ethnicity, which can also be delivered to your door. Cloning and genetic engineering, the miniaturisation of data processors and the ubiquitous – 'Can you hear me, I'm on the train?' – all-singing, all-dancing mobile phone are advances for which in the next century our own may be remembered, but there are other, lesser inventions, which our parents and grandparents managed very nicely without but which have transformed our lives.

While, ostensibly, women are no longer housewives, nurses and secretaries but round-the-world yachtsmen, CEOs and brain surgeons, has their load in any way been lightened by the fish finger (I can just see my grandmother's astonished expression in the face of 'Captain Birdseye'!), the Post-it note, the bar code, the pocket calculator (when did arithmetic go out of fashion?) or the black plastic bin bag?

Photographs in the family album reveal my grandmother in long skirts and ankle-boots over her lisle stockings, which were held up by complicated gizmos attached to her corset (made to measure by a corsetière) which cinched her waist and emphasised her bosom, while my mother, before the seductive days of 'beach and leisure wear', sported black, brown or navy-blue court shoes with matching handbags even at the seaside. Her pre-war cupboard had, I remember, row upon row of dancing shoes in satin shades of scarlet, orange or lime-green, very pointed and very high of heel, which complemented the slinky 'evening dresses' worn to fashionable joints such as the Trocadero in Piccadilly, now home, among other things, to a multiplex cinema. With the advent of the war years, from 1939 onwards, these brightly coloured outfits were abandoned (I wish I could have kept them for my granddaughters) and the dancing days rudely interrupted.

It was not until 1949, the year of my marriage, that the 'trainer', designed in Germany by one 'Adi' (Adolph) Dassier, was first registered in Germany. The widespread, unisex adoption of this comfortable footwear, originally intended for running, underscores the present relaxed attitude to dressing, the rise and rise of the leisure industry and the increasing preoccupation with fitness which began in the 1970s and peaked in the 1980s when gyms and fitness centres opened their doors, and city streets and urban parks echoed with the thump-thump of joggers, water bottles in their hands. Training shoes became big business, not simply because everyone was running around and jumping up and down in the evenings and at weekends (or *on the* weekends according to the vernacular) but because they were comfortable and made you look fit even if you never raised a sweat. Embellished with distinctive logos, the shoes achieved cult status among the young, especially in the United States, where inner-city kids were known to steal and even to kill for them. Sixty years on, the trainer, with its fashionable permutations, has joined blue jeans as the universally democratic wear for all ages and all nationalities. In my own case, suffering from peripheral neuropathy as I do, it has served another purpose. Incapable of putting my foot to the ground in anything other than its flexible upper and thick-wedged sole, it facilitates my mobility and enables me to get about.

It is a far cry from my early experiences in shops with arcane names – Daniel Neal and Lilley & Skinner – to which I was taken by my mother to buy shoes. These shoes were inevitably made by Startrite, officially the first shoemaker in Great Britain to offer a ready-made service to the public, whose James Smith, a young leather worker, started their creation in Norwich, in 1792, and who, unbelievably, are still going strong today. The company prided itself on the fact that they were the only manufacturer to make shoes that would prevent damage to children's feet. To this end many of the shops to which they were supplied employed not only skilled and motherly 'fitters' but made fulsome use of X-ray machines which, in the light of today's knowledge of the harmful effects of radiation, particularly on the very young, were an unacceptable liability that far outweighed the benefits of ensuring the best fit for impressionable feet. Like all children, I was fascinated by these cumbersome machines, which lurked in the corners of the shoe departments. Once the feet had been meticulously tabulated and carefully measured as to the correct length and width, and shoes of approximately the right size (be they 'indoor' or 'outdoor' and never the twain should be confused) and colour had been selected, the child was helped up the rubber step of the monolith and instructed to place his/her feet into the maw of the machine. The light, surreally green, was turned on and the child instructed to wriggle his/her toes now magically transformed into ten bony protuberances that could be viewed with wonder through an eyepiece, for all the world like a ship's funnel, at the top of the contraption. According to how far the ends of the toes were removed from the now easily visible semicircle of nails in the sole plate, the shoes were declared too large, too small or, according to the skill of the operator, just right.

Back then, in the mists of time, when children were children and in most cases remained so until they were well into their teens, 'sensible' Startrites – with their plethora of widths from C through to H – as the shoes of parental choice, presented few problems. Today the firm boasts several Royal Warrants and its shoes were (allegedly) worn by both Prince William and Prince Harry. Although it continues to dominate the market with its 'back-to-school' range and boasts of 'quality footbed' and 'arch support', the Miss Rhino range, for older girls, goes largely unheeded and any teenager worth her salt would far rather have a pair of 'Jimmy Choos'.

The trainer is not the only twentieth-century development with which I would like to surprise my grandparents and bamboozle my parents. While 'shopping', once a strictly 'ladies only' responsibility – no man would be seen dead doing it any more than he would be caught pushing a baby buggy (in itself a twentieth-century invention) – I wonder if it hasn't been two steps forward and one step back. While the Ocado van, at the press of a few computer buttons, delivers the week's or month's groceries to the door, in pre-war days my mother, whose shopping was done on a daily basis and occupied much of her untrammelled time, had only to telephone the butcher, the baker, the pharmacy or the greengrocer for half a dozen lamb chops, a 'bloomer', a bottle of Elliman's Embrocation or a couple of pounds of potatoes, for a boy on a bicycle to bring them to the door in brown-paper bags, sometimes within the half-hour. By the same token, although a sign on the front door read 'No hawkers, no Circulars', the Boy Scouts collected jumble and old newspapers, the dining chairs got re-caned, the knives sharpened and the coal in its heaving black sacks delivered.

The 'supermarket', second home or dating agency to some and the highlight of the week to many, with its massive car parks and 24/7 opening hours, revolutionised the way people shop and is a twentieth-century wonder in its own right. Dazzling, garish and copiously stocked with enough provisions to relieve a great deal of Third World hunger, it has become *palais de dance*, workingmen's club and bingo hall, and friendships have been forged and feuds resolved in its seemingly random but meticulously structured aisles.

To someone who remembers the days when requests for groceries were fulfilled by assistants, while customers stood patiently in front of the counter and indicated what it was they wanted from shelves advisedly out of their reach, these soulless 'hyper-markets' often a universe in themselves, represent, according to where it is you stand, either a twentieth-century blessing or a neon-lit curse.

My own impressionable years, during the Second World War, were spent queuing up for 'rations' such as the twelve ounces (what's an ounce, Granny?) of sugar and four (later two) ounces of butter and one ounce of cheese each week. This government parsimony left a legacy, greeted with good-natured hilarity by my daughters, in the shape of my habit of scraping the last morsel of butter from the paper and using it to grease an oven dish.

By the end of 1940 family store cupboards were empty. While the under fives and expectant mothers were allocated the odd orange (never having seen one before, one child ate hers with the skin on), lemons and bananas had vanished for the duration and onions – imported from the Channel Islands and Brittany – had temporarily disappeared although some rare specimens were said to have been offered as raffle prizes or even birthday presents. Tinned meat and fruit, which were not rationed, had completely gone from the shops (but were to return some months later under a 'points' scheme, sixteen points a month) with which you could choose to buy rice, condensed milk, jam, marmalade, honey, breakfast cereals, biscuits, sardines and baked beans according to your priorities. No satisfactory distribution system was ever devised for fish, which together with elusive 'offal' remained unrationed, but led to long queues (in which it was not uncommon for women to faint and to ignore the air-raid sirens for fear of losing their place) outside the fishmongers' for slabs of salted cod which had the texture of boiled flannel, a couple of herrings, a tail of hake, or whale-meat steaks, which tasted like lumps of solidified cod-liver oil. To be caught trying to get a second share of anything resulted in social disgrace.

A more serious shortage than that of fresh fruit was that of eggs; one a week, followed by one a fortnight, and later none at all, other than the unappetising 'dried egg', and a wasted egg was a major disaster, which still resonates with me to this day. While all this must have been a sore trial for my mother and grandmother (who lived with us) who had to attempt to provide wholesome meals from these paltry ingredients, the shortage which, unsurprisingly, affected me most was that of chocolate and sweets. The ration, irrespective of one's age, was eight ounces of sweets or chocolates every four weeks. Two ounces a week, although ample for the moderate sweet eater, was an appalling penance for a sweet-toothed child such as myself and hours would be spent considering the best way to 'spend' my doll-sized 'sweet coupons', which had to be painstakingly cut out (not merely cancelled) from a sheet, and it was only too easy to demolish the entire month's allowance in one glorious splurge, bearing in mind that halfpenny 'gob-stoppers' and giant 'pear drops' could be sucked for half an hour, while precious chocolate, to which I am still addicted, disappeared in moments.

Today shopping for food, like shopping for clothes, has achieved ritual rather than necessity status and the super-market complex, the latest of which boasts forty restaurants and fourteen-cinema screens, and where you can buy anything from baby food and books to financial services, cards and CDs, where, under the same roof, you can have your medicines dispensed and your car topped up with petrol, has for many families, and in many cases, become a regular place of worship. Stocked over-abundantly with meat from Mexico, cheese and foie gras from France, melons from Costa Rica, beans from Kenya, asparagus from Peru, spinach from California, peanuts from Georgia, strawberries from Israel and wines from South Africa and the New World, these temples of Mammon, these paeons of plenty with their sleep-walking congregations, have become the seductive, garish cathedrals *de nos jours*.

19

Character Arc

*There is no enterprise which is started with such tremendous
hope and high expectations and yet fails so often as love.*

ERICH FROMM

While its execution may take no more than a few hours
daily out of the twenty-four, writing is a full-time job and
every moment, even those we must of necessity spend away
from our desks, is precious. While we resent (see Chapter
17) the interruptions – despite the fact that Philip Roth says
he writes eight hours a day 365 days a year! – which life as
a human being forces upon us, there are some distractions
which, in the interests of our chosen career, we voluntarily
impose upon ourselves. One of these is to attend a Robert
McKee seminar which, gruelling as it is (of which more
later), not only inspires but reinvigorates us.

Robert McKee is a creative writing instructor who started
out playing the title role in *Martin the Shoemaker* in his
home town, Detroit, at the age of nine. Having completed
his Bachelor of Arts degree at the University of Michigan, he
toured with the APA (Association of Producing Artists) and
appeared on Broadway, before returning to Ann Arbor to

earn his Master's degree in Theater Arts. Later he travelled to London to become Artist-in-Residence at the National Theatre and studied Shakespearean production at the Old Vic, after which he returned to New York to spend the next seven years as actor/director on Broadway. Having decided to make his career in film, he attended cinema school and moved to Los Angeles, where he wrote screenplays (none of which was produced) and television scripts (including *Columbo* and *Kojak)* which were, and worked as a story analyst.

In 1983, as Fulbright scholar, McKee joined the faculty of the School of Cinema-Television at the University of Southern California, where he began offering his now famous 'Story' seminar class (see Chapter 20 of *The Writing Game).* A year later he opened the course to the public, giving a three-day, thirty-hour intensive class to sold-out audiences. Since 1984 more than 50,000 writers and wannabe writers have attended his lectures in cities around the world from Los Angeles, New York, Sydney and Helsinki to Munich, Tel Aviv, Singapore and Barcelona. Although McKee has not himself ever managed to write an award-winning script, his former students (among them actors Kirk Douglas and John Cleese) now include twenty-six Academy Award winners, 125 Emmy Award winners and sixteen Directors' Guild of America Award winners. Although not all these honours were awarded for writing, the winners had all participated in McKee's course either before, or after, receiving their awards. His best-selling book, *Story: Substance, Structure, Style and the Principles of Screenwriting,* has become required reading for film and cinema schools, and is now in its nineteenth printing in the United States and fourteenth in the UK. While both the course and the book principally address screenwriters, McKee examines the narrative structure of writing per se and analyses what it is that makes a story compelling. His theories apply equally to genres other than film and encompass any form of writing as long as it attempts to 'tell a story'.

While it was many years ago that I attended the arduous 'Story' seminar, which was held at the National Liberal Club, and I cannot put my hand on my heart and swear that I have not consciously put any of McKee's theories into practice, when I heard recently that he was coming to London with 'Love Story Day', although a 'love story' was not, as far as I was aware, on my writing agenda, I hurried to register before the course was sold out.

It is a known fact that the writer writes not about what has happened but about what is going to happen. We have no idea why we do some things and don't do others, why we write about some things and not about others. Our antennae are very finely tuned, however, and although at the time there appears no rhyme or reason for our actions, we follow our noses and, time after time, some seminal idea, some ground-breaking concept, will result.

First the man himself. If there is such a thing as 'charisma', Robert McKee has it in spades. Now approaching seventy, McKee, as do we all, has aged in the intervening years from when I last heard him speak. He is stooped, so that his crumpled linen jacket hangs loose from his shoulders; his stride is less certain as are his movements when he fusses with the height of his chair (on which he never sits), his notes, his spectacles, the silver screens on which he will later project clips from classic films – such as *Tootsie* and *Brokeback Mountain* – his trademark coffee mug, his thermos flask and the water jug with which he will sustain himself throughout the marathon day that is scheduled to run from nine in the morning until nine at night.

A consummate actor and showman, McKee begins his performance as the clock strikes nine. Standing nonchalantly at ease, his hair now grey and receding from his forehead, he interacts with his audience, warming them up, getting them on his side, although this is not necessary as it becomes evident, from the show of hands he requests, that ninety-nine per cent of the students who have travelled from the United States and Malaysia, from Kenya and Croatia, from Germany and Japan to sit at his feet, have attended one of his earlier 'Story' lectures.

Before beginning the seminar proper, McKee, as is his wont, not only briefs his audience at the University of Westminster where we meet as to the location of the 'bathrooms', but lays down a few ground rules. Cellphones and bleepers: if any of his students allows a mobile to ring during the course of the lecture – God help him. He will suffer the embarrassment of being asked to scramble his way out of his seat, make his way down the steps and up again to the podium and donate ten pounds to Robert McKee. If he has no change he is not to worry, McKee has plenty. If anyone is caught 'texting' out of the line of sight and is shopped by a neighbour, the neighbour will receive ten pounds for 'squealing' from the lecturer who will not suffer any interruption to, or distraction from, his discourse. While students are allowed to take notes on their laptops, anyone caught using his computer to browse the internet and disturb his fellow students during the course of the day may be similarly shopped. Students are not permitted to ask questions or to interrupt during the lecture but are encouraged, if there is anything which they do not understand or which they wish to ask, to buttonhole the lecturer during the breaks. Breaks, of which there are only four, three of fifteen minutes plus one hour for lunch, must be strictly observed and any student overstaying the free time and hoping to slink late into his seat will be severely dealt with. Anyone caught recording the proceedings will be instantly expelled. The students, of course, regressing to the kindergarten, not only accepted the terms but lapped them up. The lecturer cleared his throat, poured his first fix of coffee, tore open the sachet of sugar with panache, and the serious business of the day began.

Where did the man, who was no longer young, get not only his patent enthusiasm for his subject, which had not diminished since I last heard him speak, but his seemingly boundless energy? Not only to stand on his feet and talk cogently, enthusiastically and inspiringly for twelve hours but to volunteer to have his brains picked during the minimalist breaks!

Everybody loves a love story, described by Graham Greene as 'one satisfying relationship with another human being' – which, incidentally, despite his many affairs he claims never to have experienced himself – and in the love story happy endings, while not always achievable, are always desirable. Throughout history, love has manifested itself in many guises. In the idealistic age of chivalry, perpetuated by the troubadours, it was chaste, enobling and ritualistic, and courtship of the beloved was carried out according to a recognised set of ethical rules; the romantics, who recognised only one true love, with love at first sight being the preferred option, followed the heart rather than the head, until in the final analysis all obstacles to the relationship were set aside. Oscar Wilde satirised romance (*The Importance of*

Being Earnest) as did many Hollywood musicals. Romance inspired the visceral and cathartic 'blues' music ('Love for Sale', 'Make a Little Love') with its roots buried deep in American history, and in the nineteenth century swains serenaded Jeannie with the Light Brown Hair so often that it was widely reported that in the interim, Jeannie's hair had turned grey!

The timelessness of love stories – Euripides' *Alcestis,* the doomed affair of *Abelard and Héloïse,* Shakespeare's *Romeo and Juliet* (aka *West Side Story*) and *The Taming of the Shrew* (*Kiss me Kate*) – suggest that love is programmed into our DNA, which releases feel-good chemicals – dopamine and testosterone – which encourage procreation and enhance the chance of survival. While it is true that in the animal kingdom angler fish and termites mate for life, this cannot be mistaken for love.

For Sigmund Freud, who believed that perfection is unattainable, love was an ideal that cannot be reached, and many of his contemporaries dismissed romantic love as an escape from reality and labelled it 'pathological'. These gurus would have been rubbish in the movie business, which relies heavily on love, be it passionate – in which the lovers are capable of anything including murder – companionate, which is not necessarily consummated, or unconditional, which totally disregards the behaviour of the significant other.

'Romantic tragedy' (*The Night Porter, Vertigo, The Great Gatsby, Madame Bovary* and *Anna Karenina*), stories of life and death in which love is seen as an addiction, has universal appeal; 'romantic comedy', which sends up the ritual of courtship and is sometimes known as 'screwball' (*Pretty Woman, When Harry Met Sally*), with its lies and deception, its reversal of power or cases of mistaken identity, attracts younger audiences, while romantic drama (*Love in the Time of Cholera*, *Farewell to Arms*, *Private Lives*) with its stories of fidelity and infidelity will have the oldies queuing at the box office. The genres can of course be mixed (*Hannah and her Sisters*, *Love Actually*, *Prizzi's Honour*).

Today, when both social and class conflicts are passé, as is the race and colour bar, parental wishes are no longer respected, romance is the lingua franca of the internet, and sex (fuelled by readily available substances such as Ecstasy) in any permutation is there for the taking and no big deal, the love story as we once knew it poses greater challenges. As romance has gone out of the window and the only couples on the street seen holding hands are gays and seniors, where are the obstacles that stand in the way of true love and what is left for the writer to write about?

Perhaps it is significant that for the first time since Sappho was writing her love poetry more than two thousand years ago, if we want to tell a story of impediment to love, which is after all the meat of most love stories and reflects a morality we no longer recognise, we must set it in the past.

It was for this reason that in order to illustrate all that was best in the love story genre, Robert McKee chose to screen *The Bridges of Madison County* – in which a macho photographer, Robert Kincaid, wanders into the life of bored housewife and mother Francesca Johnson – a doomed and classic love affair that takes place in America, in 1960s Iowa.

Adapted from the novel of the same name by Robert Waller, *The Bridges of Madison County* tells a story of the passionate love between a man (Clint Eastwood) and a woman (Meryl Streep) that happens only once in a lifetime – if you're lucky. The couple's clandestine affair – the love they must hide both from the small-town nosy parkers and

Francesca's absent husband – is shared by the audience (a *sine qua non* of the love story) and it is their secret words and shared gestures that give energy to the relationship.

As the story unfolds against the backdrop of Francesca's farmhouse and the bridges of Madison County, photographed by Clint Eastwood when he is not photographing Meryl Streep, the two lovers demonstrate the classic rituals of romance. Gifts of flowers, starlit walks, iced tea (to cool their passion as well as their bodies) and brandy, underline the pleasure of their 'accidental' touches, shared baths, mutual grooming, laughter at 'in' jokes, and the apogee of lovemaking following a sensual dance, which goes on for three and a half minutes, a kiss which is two minutes long and finally the sex (the consummation), which connects the lovers with the rest of the world. Soulmates, at odds with the circumstances in which they find themselves, both the lovers feel that coincidence from their past lives – she was born in Bari and fate has taken him there – points to a shared destiny which, even though Francesca goes so far as to pack her cases, we all know can never be.

The passionate four-day affair in the isolated farmhouse is interrupted only by an unwelcome neighbour who stops innocently by with home baking. While the story follows its predictable course – attraction, flirtation, resistance, foreplay, surrender, consummation and afterglow – complication, in the form of the return of Francesca's fond but tedious family, and separation, is the order of the day. The climax of the movie comes with Francesca's decision not to leave her faithful but boring husband, and the resolution of it with the evidence of the *liaison amoureuse,* which she leaves for her children after her death, and the scattering of the erstwhile lovers' ashes from the bridges of Madison County.

By the end of the gruelling day, Robert McKee has revealed to us the history, the nature and the conventions of love. He has outlined the evolution, the chemistry, the psychology, the components and the three dimensions of love. He has explained the difference between character dimension, character motivation and character arc, told us about anti-empathy, or blame, about the gender divide and the forces opposed to love. He has insisted that we must choose a point of view, create the 'meet' (inciting incident), exploit the crisis, remember the resolution and work on the 'controlling idea' and that for every plot there must be one or more subplots. All this, and more, in the course of a day he has taught us, but what have we learned?

We are artists, not journeymen, and must follow not only our masters but write out of our own heads. If we are to be true to ourselves we must put away the notebooks in which we have scribbled our often incomprehensible notes, the words of wisdom as they fell from the maestro's lips, and tell our own stories. While the seminar has been fascinating, stimulating, illuminating, memorable and informative, and has given us the rare opportunity to mix with other like-minded writers, when push comes to shove, we cannot work by numbers but, like all those who have the chutzpah to create something out of nothing, must blunder into the darkness on our own. If and when, in the future, I decide to write a love story, it will come from the heart and not the head.

20

Family Reunion

*My family and I send our warmest wishes to all celebrating
the sacred festival of Passover.*

BARACK OBAMA

According to literary critic and novelist Cyril Connolly 'there
is no more sombre enemy of good art than the pram in the
hall'. This sad reflection from the overweight and unkempt
author of the seminal *Enemies of Promise,* whose spendthrift
habits, promiscuous private life and failure to produce the
masterpiece he would have liked, were, by his own admission, a series of defeats, does not bear too close a scrutiny.
While the 'pram in the hall' and its connotations undoubtedly makes serious inroads upon the (woman) writer's time
and energy, it also puts her in touch with her true nature,
and links her inextricably to the larger world. This view
was shared by best-selling writer J. G. (Jim) Ballard, a single
(widowed) parent to his three children, who swore that his
work benefited greatly from his rich family life and thought
that the 'pram in the hall', far from being a brake on creativity, was his greatest ally. It may of course be true that 'the
birth of children is the death of parents', but it is their birth,
no matter how traumatic, their presence, no matter how

imperfect, and their upbringing, no matter how thankless, that not only brings its own rewards, which are sometimes hard to see, but keeps their parents grounded and enables them to become the rounded and fulfilled human beings which in time will fuel their writing. The family, so psychologists tell us, is the foundation of all human existence. It is the nutriment of our humanness and our individuality, and family life is the bulwark of our race. With all due respect to Cyril Connolly, who was unlucky enough to have had no children of his own, the family, an institution that has been around since the dawn of history, is the acknowledged basis of all drama even though it has been described by August Strindberg, a disillusioned exponent of it, as '... the suppressed home of the virtues, where innocent children are tortured into their first falsehoods, where wills are broken by parental tyranny and self-respect smothered by jostling egos'.

The Jewish sense of family has been summarily dismissed as tribalism, yet its themes, rooted in the Bible, ensure that universal brotherhood, justice and mercy can be called upon at crucial moments in human history. While it was a mystery to Virginia Woolf – '... how any woman with a family ever put pen to paper ... Always the bell rings and the baker calls' – maternity, with which unfortunately she was unfamiliar, *is* creativity in a deeply satisfying way. If culture is something that makes life worth living, by far the most important channel of transmission remains the family, and when family life fails to play its part we can expect our culture to deteriorate. This view about the relationship between family and society is endorsed by Aristotle: 'If children did not love their parents and family members they would love no one but themselves.'

For better or worse, and for reasons which were hormonal rather than cerebral, I conceived five, and gave birth to four daughters, the youngest of whom was born when I was thirty-three (I was the oldest mother, then, outside the school gates), an age when most women today are thinking of *starting* their families. All I can say about this radical change in mores, about the tendency to delay childbearing until education and careers are established and the (more or less) correct partner found, is (boringly) that it wasn't like that in my day, when the priority was how to avoid unwanted pregnancies, and fertility treatments and in vitro fertilisation, yet to be in common usage, were neither necessary nor the norm.

While the 'bell rang and the baker called' with predictable regularity, I brought up my children, answered the door and the telephone to patients in what was then a single-handed practice, and got on with my writing. A letter from Harriet Beecher Stowe in 1850, describing the number of times she had been interrupted in her writing, revealed a soulmate:

> Since I began this note I have been called off at least a dozen times – once for the fish-man to buy a codfish – once to see a man who had brought me some baskets of apples – once to see a book man … then to nurse the baby – then into the kitchen to make a chowder for dinner and now I am at it again for nothing but deadly determination enables me ever to write – it is rowing against wind and tide.

It never occurred to me that there was any other way to write than with the cacophony of toddlers' voices competing with the muse as I sat before my typewriter, more often than not with a child on my lap. Despite today's advances, the fact that we can keep in electronic touch with friends and relatives on the far side of the world – even 'on the train' – access the latest news and the moon and produce meals in moments, I truly believe that life was easier and more stress-free in those days when we left our prams outside the shops with impunity, if a child didn't get into its first choice of school it was not a catastrophe, sell-by dates were unheard of – you used your common sense – and as far as foodstuffs were concerned we never had to read the labels because there were none.

I grow tired now even thinking how I coped with the requirements of children, both mental and physical, the demands of a marriage and the upkeep of frequently changing homes which, although it is a fact often overlooked by fifty per cent of the human race, must be managed. As if by magic, babies grow into toddlers, toddlers into children, children into schoolgirls, schoolgirls into adolescents (!), adolescents into young women, young women into brides (so it was then) and brides into mothers themselves.

Today, in the words of Margaret Thatcher, 'we are a grandmother' yet if you were to search the annals of the saccharine 'good granny' manuals ('sound on everything from nappies to tantrums') you would not find my name. I keep my silence on the received wisdom, which has changed radically since 'my day', and turn a blind eye to a two-year-old silenced with a dummy, a four-year-old still clutching a bottle, or children of various ages who erode their parents' evenings and will not go to bed. I am not interested in being an unpaid nanny or establishing myself as a 'really cool' granny willing, for the second time around, to spend my days making fairy cakes or digging sandcastles. It is not a role I aspire to. While the demands of my own children of course took precedence over my work, I am unwilling and reluctant to let my diminishing time and energy be usurped by my ten grandchildren, five girls and five boys – my daughters were cleverer than I – all of whom I love to distraction.

Of course I follow their progress, from the salad days, when they declared their intentions of becoming firemen or pink-taxi drivers, to Cambridge graduates with double firsts, actors, gymnasts, city analysts, musicians, talented chefs, special constables, aesthetes, putative vets and pirates, to men and women about town. My daughters, thankfully not in the United States or the Antipodes, all live nearby. I see my grandchildren frequently. They love coming for weekend meals or short stays, but because I am always at home and seem a natural babysitting target, the guidelines have been firmly established and their mothers know, and respect, where they must be drawn. My role is a supportive one and I am available, at the drop of my pen, for accidents and emergencies, for telephone queries and advice. I will pick up a child from school when rotas break down and feed and entertain them until they are collected by their parents. I will keep them amused for an afternoon then, usually with relief, deposit them back where they belong.

Perhaps I deceive myself about my lack of commitment to the offspring of my offspring, this youthful and reinvigorating source of so much happiness and enjoyment. I have kept all their letters, the birthday and anniversary cards sprinkled with fairy dust and signed with unsteady crayoned kisses, all their postcards in childish hands written at the instigation of parents, all their poems and their letters. Now that they are, for the most part, grown up, the relationship, without exception, is a happy one and bonds have been firmly forged. They respect my status as 'working grandmother', come, with obvious pride, to see my plays and even occasionally read my books. They mingle easily with my friends at publication parties, value my opinions, my advice and my discretion and, despite the age difference, borrow my make-up and my clothes. Until we grew too physically incompetent and they old enough to have rail cards and go backpacking with their peers, we used to take a selection of six- to fifteen-year-olds on a yearly summer holiday to a quasi 'posh' hotel. I think these few days at the English seaside were a landmark both in their lives and in ours. Away from their parents, we got to know the children better and, feeling free of restraints, they let their hair down in the knowledge that their confidences would be safe. In the old-fashioned dining room of the old-fashioned hotel – full of 'old farts' as they later reported – they learned the perennial rules of dinner-table etiquette and enjoyed ordering their meals from elaborate menus and waiters who kept their glasses filled and, coming mainly from Eastern Europe and having little English, did not laugh when the younger ones mispronounced the pretentious (French) names of the dishes.

Each year we set a competition, which everybody won and for which all received prizes: the best photographic record of the holiday, the best account, delivered to a hand-picked audience, of sights they had seen and the adventures they had had. The entry in one of the scrapbooks, from a much travelled teenager, was revealing: 'How can I sum up my holiday in Kent? The best holiday ever!' I think that says it all.

Today, despite our age, and although the number of school plays and concerts through which we have to sit proudly has dwindled and the grandchildren, mostly in their twenties and thirties, are adults making their way in the world, we remain close. We respond to their unscheduled requests to visit us, take pride in their achievements, read their tentative attempts at creative writing, applaud enthusiastically at their minor parts in off-West End plays, graciously accept their floral tokens of appreciation (even if they have been to the dead-flower stall), listen to their problems and enjoy the meals they have proudly cooked.

In 1972 the anthropologist Mary Douglas wrote about the cultural significance of meals and mealtimes. 'Deciphering a meal' demonstrated that food is just as evocative a form of communication as language. As with the words we speak or write, so the food we eat is crucially linked to the way we think about ourselves: food reveals who we are, what we might stand for and, perhaps more problematically, what we were had not the world divided us. Near or far, our homelands are reinvented and reinscribed by the food we eat.

On at least two occasions in the year the entire family – barring hard-earned acting roles or overseas work commitments – gets together. These are the holy days, Pesach (Passover) and Rosh Hashanah (the Jewish New Year). In the days of our large houses with their large dining rooms in which twenty people could be seated at a good-natured pinch, we always hosted these occasions for which I slaved for days over a hot stove and put the 'bath the baby' saucepan to good use. When we moved to an apartment the down-sized dining room, about which I was at first dubious, turned out to be an asset. Our daughters volunteered to take on the baton of the festive meals and I handed it over, not without some regret and feelings of involuntary redundancy – I had catered for and hosted these occasions for so many years – but ultimately with relief. While I had taken pride in doing every bit of shopping, every bit of preparation, every bit of cooking, myself, my four daughters, with other things on their minds, made it easy.

For Leo Tolstoy, not surprisingly, 'all happy families resemble one another, each unhappy family is unhappy in its own way.' My own mantra is that one must look at one's friends and family with 'one eye shut', in other words try to recognise and appreciate the good in everyone and, even if people don't agree with you or come up to your expectations, to try not to nit-pick.

No longer on our home ground – although by virtue of our seniority we were given the best and least constricted seats – and away from our jurisdiction, the 'family' gatherings took on a different dimension. Neither better nor worse. Just different. For one thing the catering was rationalised. All the traditional dishes that had once come out of my own kitchen were now prepared and cooked in four (when they weren't bought ready-made), with the current hostess calling the shots and working to the various strengths – the chocolate mousse maven could not roast a potato nor conjure up the historic Bakewell tart of her older sister – of her siblings, all hard-working professional women. The results were transported by willing hands, in foil-covered dishes, to be cooed over or criticised by the extended family who kept the cooks on their toes.

The apotheosis of the year was Seder Night, the Passover meal and service for which Jewish families all over the world – including many who barely acknowledged their roots – gathered together to remember the story of Exodus, the passage of their ancestors from Egypt, after 430 years of slavery, to freedom in the Land of Israel.

The Seder, with its symbols and rituals, instructs each

generation to remember their past while recognising their own freedom and the responsibilities it entails. As part of a larger global community we are urged to work to ensure that our brothers and sisters of every race, religion, culture and nationality are free from bondage and repression, and able to live in peace. It is a tall order, but at least the Seder service is a start in pointing out to those who sit (crammed) round the table that we should be thankful for the gifts that have been bestowed upon us and at the same time work to alleviate the suffering, poverty and hunger of those who are not so lucky.

It is an evening for all ages and all comers. Partaking in another's traditional fare is an acknowledged way to break down barriers and, no matter how constricted the space, it has long been the custom to invite strangers and those who would otherwise be on their own to the table. After the father's welcome, the youngest child will ask the question 'Why is this night different from all other nights?' The answers the father – from his seat at the head of the table – gives, with their traditional explanations and familiar songs, comprise the major part of the service before the festive meal, much anticipated by the restless little ones, is served.

The story kicks off with a passage about how a father must deal with his offspring (once sons, now gender-neutral in accordance with the times): a wise one, a wicked one, a foolish one and one too young to ask questions. He then explains to the assembled company the symbolism of the Seder foods, which are arranged on a special plate before him: the shank bone, symbol of the temple offerings; eggs, for spring renewal; herbs, to remind us of the bitterness of slavery; salt water for our tears and *charoset,* a sweet paste made with apples and nuts, which 'tastes like' the mortar used by the Jewish slaves.

The ensuing poems, songs, commentaries, stories and games for the children (a competition to find the *afikoman* or hidden matzoh) follow more or less the same pattern year after year. While the father may bravely attempt to introduce new readings from great or lesser poets, to bring the proceedings into the twenty-first century with sombre memories of the Holocaust, and to invite theological argument from the older members of the family, the core of the evening remains both reassuringly familiar and thought-provoking. Despite each family's idiosyncrasies, its own special customs and melodies and the fact that, for some, the annual Seder is the one remaining connection with their Jewish identity, much of what it does, together with the instruction to remember the past and be thankful for the gifts that have been bestowed upon us, would be familiar to Jewish families all over the world. With its warm ritual, its fun and its festive meal, the occasion gives people of all ages the chance to 'catch up', and even if that is the extent of their commitment they may be inspired to repeat the story to their children and they to theirs, and perhaps some future generation will hear it for the first time and want to reconnect with the past. In our own family, together with the prayers and the *Haggadah* (the illustrated book that each child proudly receives on his/her fifth birthday), it may be the time that one of the young ones was stung by a bee while searching for the *afikoman*, or the evening when a participating six-year-old pronounced the word 'psalm' as 'plasma' – provoking tears of laughter – which will be best remembered, but at least, in the interests of continuity, we will have tried.

21

The Golden Mask

This secure screener is loaned to you, the member, for viewing by you for awards consideration only. Do not copy, upload to the internet or publicly perform it. It is illegal to loan, rent, sell or give it away. Unauthorised use will lead to criminal prosecution ...

As a voting member of the British Academy of Film and Dramatic Arts (Bafta), the Christmas period – or more accurately the months of November to February – is more than usually busy. It is crunch time for the compulsory voting which culminates in the awarding of the familiar golden masks to those getting the most votes in the annual Orange British Academy Film Awards competition.

The contest is divided into two categories: 'Production' and 'Performance'. Production includes Production Design, 'have the production designer and set decorator created the most appropriate physical setting for the characters?'; Costume Design, judged on whether the costumes are period or modern, lavish or simple, many or few and whether they enhance the understanding of the characters, period and setting of the film; Music, an important dimension of any film and its overall use must be considered;

Editing, 'have the performers and performances been shown to their best advantage? Is the storytelling clear and focused? Is the film well paced?'; Cinematography – the Director of Photography collaborates with the Director and Production Designer to create the visual style of the film through the use of light, composition, backgrounds and choreography, and will interpret the Director's vision of the script on to the screen; and Special Effects, which should display artistry and creativity, be well integrated, natural and believable. 'Performance', the simpler category, encompasses Best Leading Actor, Best Leading Actress, Best Leading Supporting Actor and Best Supporting Actress, all of whom must be voted for until the contest is finally whittled down to the five overall best films from which an outright winner – the film with the most votes – is at last selected.

For the Bafta members qualified to vote, the privilege presents an awesome responsibility. Voting is compulsory and any qualified members who fail to do so lose all film voting privileges for the following year, although in a get-out clause, members may formally abstain in any single category which – owing to pressures of work or the fact that they have not seen a sufficient number of films throughout the awards year – they feel unable or unqualified to judge. Voting, a serious commitment, is carried out online and each voting member is provided with a unique user name and password, which must be entered for each round. Winning the coveted mask is the highest accolade in the industry because the recipient knows that his/her work or film has been voted for by a peer group supposedly at the top of their game. The system is designed to be as fair as possible and the results reflect the opinions of all film voting members.

The onslaught starts at the end of October or the beginning of November each year when jiffy bags, mainly from the US with a scattering from the UK, come by Fedex or DHL through the letter box or are handed in by the postman, first in a manageable trickle and later in an avalanche. While the DVDs, often in a foreign language – a separate voting category – represent films that have appeared in the past year and are designed to woo voters at home, many of the eligible movies can also be viewed at Bafta Piccadilly from the comfortable armchairs and large Dolby surround sound screen of the Princess Anne Theatre where strict Academy rules apply:

Latecomers will not be admitted.

There should be no talking during screenings.

Feet/legs should not be put on seats.

All members of the audience are asked to remain in their seats until the end of the closing credits (except in emergencies!).

Members must be considerate and polite to others and take responsibility for the behaviour of their guest(s).

Members must treat Academy staff and fellow members with courtesy and must 'swipe in' or show their membership cards to the host on duty and on request when entering the Princess Anne Theatre.

During the voting period the popularity of Bafta voting

members is at its zenith. Too lazy, too time-challenged or too poverty-stricken to go to the cinema, friends and family avail themselves of our bottomless pit of entertainment which, on pain of a $250,000 fine or a term in a federal prison, may neither be pirated nor lent to *anyone*. Each DVD is encrypted with the member's name and the threats for misuse of the privileged material are deeply serious.

During the film voting period additional perks (or clutter, depending on one's point of view) arrive in the form of free weekly copies of *The Hollywood Reporter* and *Variety*, the international entertainment magazine. As well as critical reviews of 'Golden Pics' and 'Special Reports' – 'joining the Academy isn't easy. You'd be surprised who's not a member' – and artists' agencies publicly congratulating their clients on their award nominations, one can slaver over techni-coloured details of residences, penthouses and beachfront villas offering distinguished lifestyles, spa-baths, gourmet kitchens, state-of-the-art screening rooms and infinity pools in Cabos San Lucas or Marina Del Rey. When the voting is over, not unexpectedly, the weekly supply of these techni-coloured freebies abruptly stops.

The film voting is divided into three rounds. Having made a shortlist from the movies he/she has managed to see over the year, a dozen 'best' are originally voted for. In the second round these are whittled down to five and in the third round the overall best film must be selected. While one does of course give it one's best shot, choosing a winner is some-times like comparing an omelette with last Tuesday. How can one weigh the harrowing *Boy in the Striped Pajamas* – in which the young German son of a Nazi officer befriends a Jewish inmate of a concentration camp in the Second World War and is ultimately sent to the gas chambers – against the anodyne *Mamma Mia*, a stage-to-film adaptation of a West End musical in which Meryl Streep rocks out on a Greek island to the songs of the pop group ABBA – and *Slumdog Millionaire* (the 2008 Bafta winner), with its disturbing images and language, in which an eighteen-year-old orphan from the slums of Mumbai is one question away from winning twenty million rupees on *Who Wants to Be a Millionaire?* when he is arrested by the police on suspicion of cheating?

Conscious of the privileges and responsibilities membership of Bafta imposes upon one, one does one's best and come February, when the awards are announced and presented to the recipients at the Gala ceremony, it is rewarding – and sometimes satisfying – to see if your judgement of the entries coincides with that of your fellow voters. As one's popularity with post-prandial visitors wanes, and the pile of DVDs one has managed to see towers over those one has not, your sigh of relief is echoed throughout the Bafta headquarters at 195 Piccadilly. Having done one's duty for another year, it is time to relax. Whether you agree with the choice of the final winners in the various categories is immaterial. Voting is over this time round and one never needs to buy a jiffy bag again.

February is an unattractive month and once the film voting, the New Year celebrations and the seasonal coughs and colds are over we like to sneak away to the Caribbean where 'compulsory viewing' comprises nothing more arduous than a swaying coconut palm and the therapeutic sight of the ocean. When we are asked by friends and acquaintances whose vacations are still spent wandering around museums and archaeological sites dating from 500 BC with guidebooks in their hands, or hurling themselves down a Swiss alp zipped into salopettes and wearing woolly hats, and who must have action else they would 'go mad', what there is to *see* on our island, we tell them purple-throated caribs and frigatebirds, brown-throated parakeets and laughing gulls – a far cry from the sooty pigeons of Camden Town.

When they enquire, politely, what the attraction is, we answer 'nothing'. Absolutely nothing. No sights that must be seen, no architecture that must be visited, no nightlife that must be endured. Our 'travels', so seductive in youth and middle age – when Angkor Wat and the Sagrada Familia, the Pyramids of Giza and the Museum of Antiquities in Cairo were food for the soul and the Temple of Apollo, the Acropolis and the Parthenon its libation – are largely over. We have no burning desire for churches and cathedrals, and not the slightest wish to be constantly engaged. These respites are to the year what compulsory breaks are to the day or battle duties to the army, which meticulously divides its watches and exempts those returning from an expedition from night duty. *Dolce far niente*. Science tells us that the brain is more active when apparently idling than when focused on a task. Focus shuts down most of its operations, whereas 'doing nothing' is to remember, feel, survey, realise, create. Our minds must relax sometimes and, like fertile farmland, they will not only function better but become more productive after a rest.

Lulled by the indolent lap of the warm sea against the silver sand, tuned in to the song of the yellow-breasted chats lured in their numbers by the crumbs of your breakfast, holidays are spent reading and reflecting. Physically refreshed by the clear skies and crystalline air, the only exercise we take – other than a morning swim and the walk from beach to restaurant – is to carry out an annual mental stocktaking as we remind ourselves that 'the unexamined life is not worth living'.

Our preferred choice of destination is Antigua. It is the nearest Caribbean island to the UK and can be reached in an eight-hour non-stop flight. Flying is not my (and I suspect many others') favourite mode of transport and some time ago I made a concerted effort to confront my fears, which in common with most writers I put to good use in a novel, *Rose of Jericho*:

Kitty did not like flying and the fact that she was on her own did nothing to mitigate her fears. Each time the keen of the engines diminished, her heart sank with it; each time the wide body of the jet swooped she plunged mentally earthwards, effaced for all time. She did not like to leave the safety of her seat, where she kept the belt fastened across her lap, for fear of confounding the equilibrium of the unnatural monster in which she had paid good money to be incarcerated, and was not at all happy when others walked carelessly up and down the aisles. It was not that she was afraid of dying. Since she had been a widow, since Sydney's death, she had looked upon herself as being totally dispensable, but when her time came she preferred to die comfortably – if possible in her own bed – surrounded neither by the marvels of hospital technology nor that of the cabin in the sky in which, from her window seat, she felt she had only to put out her hand to touch the passing clouds.

An audio tape 'Fearless Flying' by the American hypnotherapist Robert Farago – 'the longest journey starts with a single step' – provided some relief. Playing it several times over, I learned from the calm and soothing voice that flying was far and away the safest form of transport known to man (!), that the wings were *designed* to be flexible and wave about like palm trees, to regard the scary tone changes of the engine on take-off as nothing more than the raising of the undercarriage or withdrawal of the flaps, to view turbulence in the same way as a boat bouncing along the water and that aeroplanes DO NOT FALL OUT OF THE SKY. While I was not totally convinced by its rational arguments, the tape did mitigate some of my fears. Although I now strap myself into an aircraft seat more or less willingly, for want of an alternative form of transport to the place I want to go, I never cease to be amazed when, on the return flight, the wheels of the aircraft touch down again at Gatwick, Stansted or Heathrow.

The lure of eight nights away from the daily treadmill helps to overcome my reluctance to take the long flight to Antigua and I console myself with the fact that there is no gain without pain. Antigua, at 108 metres square, is the largest of the Leeward Islands. With temperatures ranging from the mid-seventies to the high-eighties cooled by a gentle breeze, its sweeping bays, its astonishing backdrop of hills and tropical rainforest, it is, as far as I am concerned, the nearest one can get to paradise. From the moment one lands at V. C. Bird airport (Papa Bird, the colony's first Chief Minister, later accused of 'unbridled corruption'), the hurly and the burly of one's daily life fall away, cares fade, the mind is indulged and the body geared for a week of barefoot inertia. There are attractions on the island should one feel so disposed: military fortifications left behind by the British who ruled Antigua for more than three centuries; English Harbour and Nelson's Dockyard, the key facility for the British navy who once ruled the waves and now a haven for visiting yachts; a National Museum (thirty minutes max!), the bustling, potholed (take your life in your hands) sidewalks of the sweltering capital, St John's, home to visiting cruise ships bringing their daily boatloads of souvenir shoppers, and, of course, cricket, the national pastime. After several visits to the island it is a case of having dutifully 'been there' and 'done that', and we are now content to enjoy a diet of the sweet indigenous 'black' pineapples, local mangoes and sapodillas, of exotic vegetables, 'pepperpot stew' and red snapper, of grouper and mahi-mahi as, prostrate on the breeze-cooled beach, we make inroads into the reading matter that has accounted for the weight of much of our luggage.

Selecting holiday reading is no trivial matter. It is as important as is an adequate supply of sun cream or packing the right clothes. According to Harold Nicolson, diplomat, author, diarist, politician and husband of Vita Sackville-West, who knew a thing or two about books: 'The test of whether you enjoy reading is a simple one. If you leave your home and you take your own book with you, it means that you are one of those who read sincerely. If, on the other hand, when you leave your home you rely either on the railway bookstall or on the books which you may or may not find there, when you arrive, it means that you do not care for reading.'

Novelist Arnold Bennett put it somewhat more succinctly: 'The man who does not read books is merely not born. He can't see, he can't hear; he can't feel in any full sense, he can only eat his dinner.' While the week in Antigua fortunately enables us to enjoy both books and dinner, the decision about which of the former to pack has taken weeks, or even months, before the holiday when a list is made, choices whittled down and Amazon put on red alert. While for writer and columnist Bernard Levin – his career curtailed by the early onslaught of Alzheimer's disease – 'the deepest pleasure of reading comes from books that do nothing useful for us', Anthony Burgess considered the passion for reading the 'greatest gift': '… it consoles, it distracts, it excites, it gives you knowledge of the world and experience of a wide kind. It is a moral illumination.'

Like a box of assorted chocolates, holiday reading matter must reflect every mood, the only caveat being that the books, if they are in hardback, should not be too heavy. Holding up a densely printed and cumbersome tome while lying horizontal on a sun lounger will defeat the object of the holiday, which is certainly not to put an unnecessary strain on both the biceps and the eyes. From the pile on the table of the Ocean Suite – from which one can step directly on to the beach – according to one's disposition, a volume is chosen and the day's expectations indulged as the latest Man Booker Prize-winner vies with a much-loved 'oldie', the philosopher with the entertainer, the ephemeral with the reassuring classic. If one has not got one's sums right and the days of the holiday outnumber the words on the page, disaster ensues.

Our favourite hotel boasts a 'library' – as well as a screening room where movies, all of which thanks to Bafta I have of course seen, are offered nightly – from which books may be borrowed, but this is not the same. While the eclectic choice is not to be sneezed at – books on art and photography, romantic and detective novels, travel guides and a miscellany of well-thumbed paperbacks left behind by guests – it is not the same as the carefully chosen nutriment one has brought with one for the mind. It was Benjamin Disraeli who said, 'If I want to read a book I write one', and with the reading matter exhausted it is time to stare at the ocean and with the brain switched off and no work or domestic trivia to interrupt the tranquillity of the sun-kissed day, to let the thoughts arrive. The pencil, with which I have annotated the books I have read, and the spiral-bound notebook, without which I never leave home, are put to good use. Ideas, themes and plots for stories, for novels and for plays vie with each other for attention and the one that remains at the top of the queue when I return home to the empty fridge, the backlog of post and the hundreds of emails crying out for my attention is the one for which, once again at my computer as if I had never left, I will create a new 'folder', the contents of which will occupy me until the next trip to Nirvana and the attainment of beatitude.

22

Feeling and Thinking

A man who gives a good account of himself is probably lying …
GEORGE ORWELL

'Life is a sexually transmitted disease with a hundred per cent mortality.' We all feel we are immortal, yet we all know we are going to die. This dichotomy has fuelled the output of poets, dredging their souls for verse, and songsters cashing in on the potent appeal of cheap music. At the beginning of the nineteenth century John Keats wrote: 'When I have fears that I may cease to be / Before my pen has glean'd my teeming brain …' and a hundred years later Frank Sinatra (who had regrets, while Edith Piaf had none) expressed his fears of mortality in an attempt to exorcise them as he made love to the microphone and confessed that he 'faced the final curtain …'

On 12 October 2006, his seventy-seventh birthday, Magnús Magnússon, the presenter of *Mastermind*, the popular television programme, was diagnosed with pancreatic cancer. He noted mordantly that 'this has to be one of the worst birthdays ever'. He died from the disease on 7 January one year later, to be outlived by his brave catchphrase 'I've

started so I'll finish'. But had he finished? Or did he feel, like
so many of us, that his life was coming to an end just when
he was getting ready for it?

Cancer is a funny thing and the recent revelation of
author and playwright Simon Gray's lung cancer (which
paradoxically was not the *coup de grâce* that killed him),
and the prostate cancer – now almost a cliché in ageing men
– which got the better of best-selling author J. G. Ballard,
produced sadness but little shock. Do artists get better
with age? While Wordsworth's declining years were largely
unproductive, Beethoven went from strength to strength
with his late quartets. Some writers, such as Philip Larkin
in his fifties and T. S. Eliot who managed to stop just in
time, voluntarily throw in the towel early, and others, such
as Gabriel García Márquez, Kingsley Amis, Graham Greene
and Evelyn Waugh, struggle on but produce work that is less
than noteworthy (embarrassingly *un*noteworthy in the case
of Márquez in whose latest novel a pathetic old man lusts
after an adolescent virgin in an attempt to recapture his lost
youth) others, such as Philip Roth, once the *enfant terrible*
of American fiction, using age to fuel his writing, go from
strength to strength.

For both writers and actors life is still not exactly 'a
country for old men'. Many erstwhile male film stars, refusing to languish in homes for aged thesps or bore the pants
off anyone they can find with richly embroidered accounts
of their early screen exploits, have managed either to turn
their careers to their advantage or, as they approach the final
hurdle and before they resemble Yeats's 'tattered coat upon
a stick', to turn them round. Swallowing their pride, they
embrace the roles of old codgers (Jack Nicolson and Morgan
Freeman in *The Bucket List,* and Michael Caine, a grumpy

old bastard who is tossed into a clapped-out nursing home in the movie *Is There Anyone There?*) or, like the unashamedly ageing Clint Eastwood who acts his socks off in *Gran Torino* and makes no attempt to hide his wrinkles, use their wisdom and insight and take up the challenge of directing. Women in the movie business know that any halfway decent parts for the over-forties are few and far between, and that it is a truth universally acknowledged that any movie in which a female protagonist, let alone an ageing one, has to carry the starring role will attract neither finance nor the Hollywood green light.

Death (if not life) and the gaze of the night (if not the blindness of the day) tell us that experience is limited, all art, by its very nature, is imperfect and no artist is ever completely fulfilled. Seeking immortality through her work, the film actress, like the writer and the artist, is doomed to disappointment. While in our mind's eye we will always see Greta Garbo, the embodiment of the Hollywood star system, as Anna Karenina, or Queen Christina gazing wistfully from the prow of the ship that delivers her from passionate love to impassioned memory, we know that Greta Gustafsson will never make another movie.

Women writers, immune to 'prostateland', have it easier. Like the inexhaustible P. D. James, who at ninety is thinking about her next novel, and Nobel Prize-winner Doris Lessing who has only just given up, they can carry on until the ideas cease to flow and the brain cells cease to function. It is the publishers, in their perennial quest for debut authors whom they can 'build up' (i.e. make money out of), who put the lid firmly on many a still-bubbling cauldron and, unable to find an outlet for their work, there is nothing left for many ageing writers but to be put out to grass or keep their minds active by joining the Open University or the University of the Third Age.

According to Henry Moore, 'the secret of life is to have a task, something you devote your entire life to, something you bring everything to, every minute of the day for your whole life. And the most important thing is, it must be something you cannot possibly do.' We are not all as lucky as the brain scientist and Nobel Laureate, Dr Rita Levi-Montalcini, who recently put her longevity down to 'no food, no husband, no regrets' and revealed that, at the age of a hundred, she was not only 'still writing' but 'still' planning another book while actively campaigning for the rights of women in Africa. While the pessimistic doctor thought that the human race was heading towards extinction and that the end was already nigh, she considered her mental acuity to be better than when she was twenty and denied that she ever grew tired of life. Uninterested in food or sleep – she gets up at five a.m. and has just one meal a day – and ignoring the role presumably played by her genes in her longevity, she said that while the secret of life was to keep thinking, we should not keep thinking about ourselves.

To our children we are always a hundred, but if we all lived to be that age there would be no room or resources on the planet for the newborn and, as I look around me, the case seems to be that under such circumstances there are very few of us who would still have whatever wits we once possessed about us, be able to avoid the humiliations of ageing and at the same time remain physically fit. There are those who truly believe that old age, with its liberation from family and other commitments, can provide leisure for you to do the things you've always wanted to do. The unwelcome corollary is that in order to enjoy this leisure to the full you also have to have both a modicum of health and a modicum of money. Sadness, the regret that one's life is finished, that one's failures remain indelible and one's successes illusory, is part and parcel of the ageing process just as, despite the best efforts of cosmetics and plastic surgery, is degeneration.

As you get older you might as well come to terms with the fact that there's no way you're going to win the Nobel Prize for Literature (described by T. S. Eliot as a 'ticket to one's own funeral', because nobody has ever done anything after he got it!), that your French will *never* be fluent and – clearly as you might picture yourself cutting a dash in the swimming pool – you're not going to master a halfway decent crawl. In the country of the old some of us have it better than others and we are lucky that although we have our freedom passes there is as yet no compulsory retirement age for writers and artists. It is paradoxical that in both these professions, just as we begin to get a clearer understanding of the human condition and its impact on our work, the arc of life is reaching its completion. Henry James might have euphemistically referred to age as 'the distinguished thing' but as anyone past their sell-by date will tell you there is nothing the least distinguished about growing old. A government survey informs us, and the Monday morning post-office queues confirm, that the fastest-growing sector of the British population is the 'oldest old', while the fastest shrinking is the youngest young.

While Balzac saw the novel as a text that gives permanence and content to all the things that resist having permanence and content, i.e. the brevity of life and material possessions, perhaps the sign of a great writer is to quit while he's ahead. According to Gabriel García's agent, the eighty-two-year-old Columbian writer is unlikely to produce another work, and Sir Vidia Naipaul, while predicting – like many other writers before him – the 'death of the novel', has intimated (possibly in a fit of pique) that he has had enough of fiction. 'I am having trouble with fiction. Why write it? I don't see why we don't write about what we feel and what we see ...'

The reality of death is that, close our eyes to its inevitability, sidestep it as we may, none of us can avoid it. Attention should perhaps be paid to the last words of Socrates at his trial: 'Now the hour to part has come. I go to die, you go to live. Which of us goes to the better lot is known to no one except the god.' Clinging to the good hope that 'death is a blessing', he had this to say to his persecutors: 'To fear death, gentlemen, is no other than to think oneself wise when one is not, to think one knows what one does not know.'*

Be that as it may, old age and its ultimate consequence presents a series of challenges, which we deal with in various ways. According to our dispositions we ignore it, capitalise on it, write a novel about it, make a film about it, buy spells to stave it off, take vitamins to delay it, invest in anti-ageing creams in the hope of concealing it, make provision for it, accept it, or shut our eyes to it and pretend it isn't going to happen. While the more pragmatic of us downsize our homes, put our affairs in order, make our wills, dispose of our valuables and make provision for our funerals down to the last details – Mozart's Requiem or Max Bruch's Violin Concerto – the more insouciant buy sports cars, squander their children's inheritance on foreign holidays in which they visit their favourite haunts for the 'last time', take up flamenco dancing or seek out new and fulfilling relationships through the columns of *The Oldie*.

---

* Apology 32

A recent survey revealed that people have at most three good 'friends' (although their circle of acquaintances may number thirty-six). When we are no longer young and just as we are forced to strike off the names of our friends in our address books, we find that we need them more than ever. As our personal landscape changes we discover that there is more pain in lost friends than in cynicism. For Seneca, 'No man is more frail than another / No man more certain of tomorrow.' Am I afraid of dying? Yes and no. My inclination is to go along with Emma Bovary: 'There's not much in dying. I shall go to sleep and it will all be over.'

For the artist, art is the best way to fight the years. I know that my work will be nowhere near finished by the time the 'fat lady sings' and I sincerely hope, as the end approaches, to be able to answer 'yes' to the question 'are you still writing?' Among the folders on my computer there is one labelled 'expectations'. It is what keeps me going. In it there are three entries: 1) ? Magna Large Print ed. early novels; 2) ? Eng. Lang. re-issue *Aristide*; 3) ? *An Eligible Man* tour.

Although eleven of my twenty novels have already been published in large print editions, eight of them have until now slipped through the net. A recent generous and unexpected offer from Magna Large Print books to publish four of the remaining titles – one of them first published forty-two years ago! – represents the success of number 1 in my list. The outcome of number 2, *Aristide*, one of my two books for children, which has already seen several reprints, was less happy. Having initially reacted enthusiastically, kept the book for several months and declared '… both myself and our reader think that *Aristide* has ongoing charm, good plot and lovely illustrations …' the assistant editor of Hodder Children's Books wrote:

We had our meeting yesterday afternoon … and I'm afraid it's not good news … As you are probably aware, the market is very difficult at the moment and we are having to be very selective. Stand-alone books are notoriously difficult to get attention for. This is obviously disappointing and I'm sorry we couldn't take things further for you, but may I say how charmed I was by Aristide and how much I enjoyed the narrative voice you employed for the story. All the best in getting your work placed elsewhere …

Expectation for an extended life for my third play, *An Eligible Man*, which has already had a successful run, is taking longer to come to fruition. My hopes were raised by Brian Russell Daniels, owner of the New End Theatre, Hampstead, where *An Eligible Man* was first produced, who thought that, with the right casting, the piece would be an 'excellent play to tour' and he is keen to organise a commercial production. To this end he asked that a script be sent to Ian Dickens of Ian Dickens Productions Ltd, the largest touring drama company in the UK. Looking up Ian Dickens on the faithful Google, I discovered that five or six of his company's productions are on at various major British theatres at any given time of the year and that these included such hardy perennials as *Rattle of a Simple Man*, *Dangerous Liaisons*, *A Woman of No Importance* and *Abigail's Party*. If anything were to come of the proposed tour, *An Eligible Man* would be in excellent company. Producer Ian Dickens was 'very keen' on the script and, five months later, it is not only still 'under serious consideration' but theatres such as the Mercury in Colchester, the Everyman in Cheltenham, the Yvonne Arnaud in Guildford, the Theatre Royal in Windsor, the Gordon Craig Theatre in Stevenage and the Capitol Theatre in Horsham have been pencilled in. Budgets are being put together to make sure the play would work financially and names such as Nigel Havers for the title role are being bandied about. The upside of the negotiations is that while the responses on the artistic side are extremely favourable, the downside, as far as the all-important finances are concerned, is the current credit crunch. As I write, the chances of a tour for *An Eligible Man* are 50:50, but the jury is still out.

So what's new? You win some and you lose some. The favourable outcome of the 'expectations' folder to date is (almost) 2 out of 3. Could one regard this as success or merely another of George Orwell's 'series of defeats', which is the writer's lot? If the plans for *An Eligible Man* come to fruition I can look forward to seeing parts of the UK I would not normally visit and revelling in audiences who would (I hope) appreciate my work. Applause is the writer's personal laurel wreath, it is what we live for. If, and when, details are settled, the play is put on – everything in the writing game historically takes a very long time – and the first night comes round, I trust that my seat will not be 'in the gods'! If it is I hope it will be a good one. If not, as they close the final curtain, I hope that I will be able to say with 'Old Blue Eyes':

I've lived a life that's full –
I've travelled each and every highway,
And more, much more than this,
I did it my way …

FINIS …
… OR NOT.

Acknowledgements

I would like to thank Prof. Andrew Lister, Emma Friedman, Ilsa Yardley, Anthony Saunders, Gary Pulsifer, Daniela de Groote, Angeline Rothermundt, James Nunn, and my husband Dennis Friedman for their invaluable help with this book.